# The Creation
# of Consciousness

Marie-Louise von Franz, Honorary Patron

**Studies in Jungian Psychology
by Jungian Analysts**

Daryl Sharp, General Editor

# The
# Creation
# of
# Consciousness

## Jung's Myth for Modern Man

## Edward F. Edinger

The material presented here first appeared in *Quadrant* (Journal of the C.G. Jung Foundation for Analytical Psychology, New York), in 1975, 1977, 1979 and 1983.

**Canadian Cataloguing in Publication Data**

Edinger, Edward F. (Edward Ferdinand), 1922-
  The creation of consciousness

(Studies in Jungian psychology by Jungian analysts; 14)

Includes index.

ISBN 0-919123-13-9

1. Psychology and religion.   2. Consciousness.
3. Jung, C. G. (Carl Gustav), 1875-1961.   I. Title.
II. Series.

BF51.E34 1984     150.19'54     C84-098147-3

INNER CITY BOOKS
Box 1271, Station Q, Toronto, Canada M4T 2P4
Telephone (416) 927-0355

Honorary Patron: Marie-Louise von Franz.
Publisher and General Editor: Daryl Sharp.


INNER CITY BOOKS was founded in 1980 to promote the understanding and practical application of the work of C.G. Jung.

*Cover:* Front face of the Bollingen stone carved by C.G. Jung. It is an eye. The little figure in the center is the *pupilla* (yourself) which you see in the pupil of another's eye. The Greek inscription, translated by Jung, reads: "Time is a child—playing like a child—playing a board game—the kingdom of the child. This is Telesphoros, who roams through the dark regions of this cosmos and glows like a star out of the depths. He points the way to the gates of the sun and to the land of dreams." (*Memories, Dreams, Reflections,* p. 227) For a transcription of the original Greek, see below, page 114.

Index by Daryl Sharp.

Printed and bound in Canada by
University of Toronto Press Incorporated

# CONTENTS

*See last pages for descriptions of other INNER CITY BOOKS*

*Where there is no vision
the people perish.*
—Proverbs 29:18.

C.G. Jung
1875-1961

(Jung at the age of 83; photo by Karsh of Ottawa)

# 1

# The New Myth

*The myth of the necessary incarnation of God...
can be understood as man's creative confrontation
with the opposites and their synthesis in the self,
the wholeness of his personality.... That is the
goal... which fits man meaningfully into the
scheme of creation and at the same time confers
meaning upon it.*
—C. G. Jung, *Memories, Dreams, Reflections.*

History and anthropology teach us that a human society cannot long survive unless its members are psychologically contained within a central living myth. Such a myth provides the individual with a reason for being. To the ultimate questions of human existence it provides answers which satisfy the most developed and discriminating members of the society. And if the creative, intellectual minority is in harmony with the prevailing myth, the other layers of society will follow its lead and may even be spared a direct encounter with the fateful question of the meaning of life.

It is evident to thoughtful people that Western society no longer has a viable, functioning myth. Indeed, all the major world cultures are approaching, to a greater or lesser extent, the state of mythlessness. The breakdown of a central myth is like the shattering of a vessel containing a precious essence; the fluid is spilled and drains away, soaked up by the surrounding undifferentiated matter. Meaning is lost. In its place, primitive and atavistic contents are reactivated. Differentiated values disappear and are replaced by the elemental motivations of power and pleasure, or else the individual is exposed to emptiness and despair. With the loss of awareness of a transpersonal reality (God), the inner and outer anarchies of competing personal desires take over.

The loss of a central myth brings about a truly apocalyptic condition and this is the state of modern man. Our poets have long recognized this fact. Yeats gave it stark expression in his poem, "The Second Coming":

> Turning and turning in the widening gyre
> The falcon cannot hear the falconer;
> Things fall apart; the centre cannot hold;
> Mere anarchy is loosed upon the world.
> The blood-dimmed tide is loosed, and everywhere
> The ceremony of innocence is drowned;
> The best lack all conviction, while the worst
> Are full of passionate intensity.
>
> Surely some revelation is at hand;
> Surely the Second Coming is at hand.
>
> The Second Coming! Hardly are those words out
> When a vast image out of *Spiritus Mundi*
> Troubles my sight: somewhere in the sands of the desert
> A shape with lion body and the head of a man
> A gaze blank and pitiless as the sun,
> Is moving its slow thighs, while all about it
> Reel shadows of the indignant desert birds.
> The darkness drops again; but now I know
> That twenty centuries of stony sleep
> Were vexed to nightmare by a rocking cradle,
>
> And what rough beast, its hour come round at last,
> Slouches towards Bethlehem to be born?[1]

This poem, first published in 1921, is astonishing in the way it succinctly strikes the major themes concerning the current state of the collective psyche. The magic circle of our mandala has broken and meaning has escaped. The falcon ego has lost the link with its creator, releasing primitive levels of the un-

---

1. W. B. Yeats, *The Collected Poems of W. B. Yeats* (New York: Macmillan Co., 1956), p. 184.

conscious from control. The ensuing chaos calls forth in compensation the birth of a new central psychic dominant. What will it be? Antichrist? The allusion to the Sphinx suggests that we must once again face the riddle of the Sphinx and ask ourselves most seriously, "What is the meaning of life?"

It is the loss of our containing myth that is the root cause of our current individual and social distress, and nothing less than the discovery of a new central myth will solve the problem for the individual and for society. Indeed, a new myth is in the making and C.G. Jung was keenly aware of that fact. A Jungian analyst once had the following dream:

> A temple of vast dimensions was in the process of being built. As far as I could see—ahead, behind, right and left—there were incredible numbers of people building on gigantic pillars. I, too, was building on a pillar. The whole building process was in its very beginning, but the foundation was already there, the rest of the building was starting to go up, and I and many others were working on it.

Jung was told this dream and his remark was "Yes, you know, that is the temple we all build on. We don't know the people because, believe me, they build in India and China and in Russia and all over the world. That is the new religion. You know how long it will take until it is built? . . . about six hundred years."[2]

Jung was the first to formulate the problem of modern man as mythlessness. As with so many of his discoveries, he found it first of all in himself. In *Memories, Dreams, Reflections* he describes that after the publication of *The Psychology of the Unconscious* in 1912[3] he had a moment of unusual clarity:

2. Max Zeller, "The Task of the Analyst," *Psychological Perspectives,* 6 (Spring 1975), p. 75.

3. The first English edition appeared in 1916. This was later revised and published as *Symbols of Transformation,* CW 5. [CW—*The Collected Works of C. G. Jung* (Bollingen Series XX). Trans. R. F. C. Hull. Ed. H. Read, M. Fordham, G. Adler, Wm. McGuire (Princeton: Princeton University Press, 1953-1979).]

"Now you possess a key to mythology and are free to unlock all the gates of the unconscious psyche." But then something whispered in me, "Why open all the gates?" And promptly the question arose of what, after all, I had accomplished. I had explained the myths of peoples of the past; I had written a book about the hero, the myth in which man has always lived. But in what myth does man live nowadays? In the Christian myth, the answer might be. "Do *you* live in it?" I asked myself. To be honest, the answer was no. For me, it is not what I live by. "Then do we no longer have any myth?" "No, evidently we no longer have any myth." "But then what is your myth—the myth in which you do live?" At this point the dialogue with myself became uncomfortable, and I stopped thinking. I had reached a dead end.[4]

Jung later found his myth, and it is the thesis of this book that just as Jung's discovery of his own mythlessness paralleled the mythless condition of modern society, so Jung's discovery of his own individual myth will prove to be the first emergence of our new collective myth. In fact, it is my conviction that as we gain historical perspective it will become evident that Jung is an epochal man. I mean by this a man whose life inaugurates a new age in cultural history.

The epochal man is the first to experience and to articulate fully a new mode of existence. His life thus takes on an objective, impersonal meaning. It becomes a paradigm, the prototypical life of the new age and hence exemplary. Jung was aware of this fact concerning his own life. Speaking of his confrontation with the unconscious he writes, "It was then that I ceased to belong to myself alone, ceased to have the right to do so. From then on my life belonged to the generality."[5]

The fact that Jung's personal life belonged to the generality was demonstrated by the uncanny parallelism between the critical episodes of his inner life and the collective crises of

4. C. G. Jung, *Memories, Dreams, Reflections* (New York: Pantheon Books, 1963), p. 171.
5. Ibid., p. 192.

Western civilization. His first major confrontation with the unconscious occurred simultaneously with the collective catastrophe of World War I.[6] From 1914 to 1918 while the nations of Western Christendom were engaged in a brutal external conflict, Jung endured the inner equivalent of the World War, withstanding and integrating the upheaval of the collective unconscious from within. William James had called for a "moral equivalent of war."[7] Jung achieved a psychological equivalent of war by which the conflict of the opposites was contained within the individual psyche. Again during World War II, Jung had his supreme revelation of the unconscious, his visions of the *coniunctio,* at the time of a grave illness in 1944.[8] By D-Day (June 6, 1944), although still hospitalized, he was well into convalescence.[9]

Almost all the important episodes of Jung's life can be seen as paradigmatic of the new mode of being which is the consequence of living by a new myth. This is not the place to examine Jung's life as a paradigm; we must instead consider the nature of the new myth which he discovered and which released him from his mythless condition.

Jung got a glimpse of his new myth while visiting the Pueblo Indians in the southwestern United States in the early part of 1925. He succeeded in gaining the confidence of Mountain Lake, a chief of the Taos Pueblos. In *Memories, Dreams, Reflections* Jung describes his conversation with Mountain Lake:

[Mountain Lake said] "The Americans want to stamp out our religion. Why can they not let us alone? What we do, we do not only for ourselves but for the Americans also. Yes, we do it for the whole world. Everyone benefits by it."

6. Ibid., pp. 175-181.
7. William James, *Essays of Faith and Morals* (New York: Longmans Green & Co., 1947), pp. 311 ff.
8. Jung, *Memories, Dreams, Reflections,* pp. 289-298.
9. Barbara Hannah, *Jung: His Life and Work* (New York: G. P. Putnam's Sons, 1976), p. 284.

I could observe from his excitement that he was alluding to some extremely important element of his religion. I therefore asked him: "You think, then, that what you do in your religion benefits the whole world?" He replied with great animation, "Of course. If we did not do it, what would become of the world?" And with a significant gesture he pointed to the sun.

I felt that we were approaching extremely delicate ground here, verging on the mysteries of the tribe. "After all," he said, "we are a people who live on the roof of the world; we are the sons of Father Sun, and with our religion we daily help our father to go across the sky. We do this not only for ourselves, but for the whole world. If we were to cease practicing our religion, in ten years the sun would no longer rise. Then it would be night forever."

I then realized on what the "dignity," the tranquil composure of the individual Indian, was founded. It springs from his being a son of the sun; his life is cosmologically meaningful, for he helps the father and preserver of all life in his daily rise and descent.[10]

This belief of the Pueblos that they help their father, the sun, to rise each day and make his transit of the heavens turns out to be a primitive, naive version of Jung's new myth. Later in 1925, while traveling in Africa, Jung had another experience that crystallized the formulation of the myth more explicitly. Jung writes:

From Nairobi we used a small ford to visit the Athi Plains, a great game preserve. From a low hill in this broad savanna a magnificent prospect opened out to us. To the very brink of the horizon we saw gigantic herds of animals: gazelle, antelope, gnu, zebra, warthog, and so on. Grazing, heads nodding, the herds moved forward like slow rivers. There was scarcely any sound save the melancholy cry of a bird of prey. This was the stillness of the eternal beginning, the world as it had always been, in the state of non-being; for until then no one had been present to know that it was this world. I walked away from my companions until I had put them out of sight, and savored the feeling of being entirely alone. There I was now, the first

10. Jung, *Memories, Dreams, Reflections,* pp. 251-252.

human being to recognize that this was the world, but who did not know that in this moment he had first really created it.

There the cosmic meaning of consciousness became overwhelmingly clear to me. "What nature leaves imperfect, the art perfects," say the alchemists. Man, I, in an invisible act of creation put the stamp of perfection on the world by giving it objective existence. This act we usually ascribe to the Creator alone, without considering that in so doing we view life as a machine calculated down to the last detail, which, along with the human psyche, runs on senselessly, obeying foreknown and predetermined rules. In such a cheerless clockwork fantasy there is no drama of man, world, and God; there is no "new day" leading to "new shores," but only the dreariness of calculated processes. My old Pueblo friend came to mind. He thought that the *raison d'être* of his pueblo had been to help their father, the sun, to cross the sky each day. I had envied him for the fullness of meaning in that belief, and had been looking about without hope for a myth of my own. Now I knew what it was, and knew even more: that man is indispensable for the completion of creation; that, in fact, he himself is the second creator of the world, who alone has given to the world its objective existence—without which, unheard, unseen, silently eating, giving birth, dying, heads nodding through the millions of years, it would have gone on in the profoundest night of non-being down to its unknown end. Human consciousness created objective existence and meaning, and man found his indispensable place in the great process of being.[11]

In *Answer to Job* he puts it more succinctly: "Existence is only real when it is conscious to somebody. That is why the Creator needs conscious man even though, from sheer unconsciousness, he would like to prevent him from becoming conscious."[12] And later, "Whoever knows God has an effect on him."[13] In his autobiography he writes:

11. Ibid., pp. 255-256.
12. C. G. Jung, *Psychology and Religion: West and East,* CW 11, par. 575.
13. Ibid., par. 617.

Man's task is ... to become conscious of the contents that press upward from the unconscious. Neither should he persist in his unconsciousness nor remain identical with the unconscious elements of his being, thus evading his destiny, which is to create more and more consciousness. As far as we can discern, the sole purpose of human existence is to kindle a light in the darkness of mere being. It may even be assumed that just as the unconscious affects us, so the increase in our consciousness affects the unconscious.[14]

And finally:

Once [the union of opposites] has been experienced, the ambivalence in the image of a nature-god or Creator-god ceases to present difficulties. On the contrary, the myth of the necessary incarnation of God—the essence of the Christian message —can then be understood as man's creative confrontation with the opposites and their synthesis in the self, the wholeness of his personality. The unavoidable internal contradictions in the image of a Creator-god can be reconciled in the unity and wholeness of the self as the *coniunctio oppositorum* of the alchemists or as a *unio mystica*. In the experience of the self it is no longer the opposites "God" and "man" that are reconciled, as it was before, but rather the opposites within the God-image itself. That is the meaning of divine service, of the service which man can render to God, that light may emerge from the darkness, that the Creator may become conscious of His creation, and man conscious of himself.

That is the goal, or one goal, which fits man meaningfully into the scheme of creation, and at the same time confers meaning upon it. It is an explanatory myth which has slowly taken shape within me in the course of the decades. It is a goal I can acknowledge and esteem, and which therefore satisfies me.[15]

These are the chief statements Jung has made concerning the emerging new myth. To many, especially those without personal experience of the unconscious, these statements may

14. Jung, *Memories, Dreams, Reflections,* p. 326.
15. Ibid., p. 338.

be hard to comprehend. The remainder of this chapter will be an effort to make the new myth somewhat more understandable. The essential new idea is that *the purpose of human life is the creation of consciousness.* The key word is "consciousness." Unfortunately, the experiential meaning of this term is almost impossible to convey abstractly. As with all fundamental aspects of the psyche it transcends the grasp of the intellect. An oblique, symbolic approach is therefore required.

I treat the idea of consciousness more fully in the next chapter. There I speak of the etymology of the word (page 36), from which we learn that consciousness and conscience are related and that the experience of consciousness is made up of two factors, "knowing" and "withness," i.e., knowing in the presence of an "other," in a setting of twoness. Symbolically, the number two refers to the opposites. We thus reach the conclusion that consciousness is somehow born out of the experience of opposites. As we shall see, the same conclusion is reached by other means.

I understand consciousness to be a substance, a psychic material usually but not always invisible and intangible to the senses. The problem in understanding concerns the words *psyche and psychic*. Until one has experienced the reality of the psyche, he can follow the discussion no further. Given the experience of psychic reality one can grasp the idea of a psychic *substance.* All psychic contents have substance, so to speak, if they are experienced as objectively real. What then distinguishes the psychic substance of consciousness? Consciousness is psychic substance connected to an ego. Or, more precisely, psychic contents which are potential entities become actualized and substantial when they make connection with an ego, i.e., when they enter an individual's conscious awareness and become an accepted item of that individual's personal responsibility.

The process whereby a series of psychic contents—complexes and archetypal images—make connection with an ego and thereby generate the psychic substance of consciousness is called *the process of individuation.* This process has as its most characteristic feature the encounter of opposites, first experienced as the ego and the unconscious, the I and the not-I, subject and object, myself and the "other." Thus we can say that whenever one is experiencing the conflict between contrary attitudes or when a personal desire or idea is being contested by an "other," either from inside or outside, the possibility of creating a new increment of consciousness exists.

Experiences of inner or outer conflict which are resolved creatively and are accompanied by a sense of satisfaction and life enhancement are examples of the creation of consciousness. Such encounters, sought deliberately and reflected upon systematically, are an essential feature of the individuation process which is a continual *auseinandersetzung* or coming to terms with contents that are "other" than or opposite to the ego. In alchemy the Philosophers' Stone is described as the mediator between opposites. In one text, where the Stone has a feminine quality, it says:

> I am the mediatrix of the elements, making one to agree with another; that which is warm I make cold, and the reverse; that which is dry I make moist, and the reverse; that which is hard I soften, and the reverse. I am the end and my beloved is the beginning. I am the whole work and all science is hidden in me.[16]

Understood psychologically, this text tells us that in the process of creating consciousness we shall at first be thrown back and forth between opposing moods and attitudes. Each time the ego identifies with one side of a pair of opposites the unconscious will confront one with its contrary. Gradually, the individual becomes able to experience opposite viewpoints simultaneously. With this capacity, alchemically speaking, the Philosophers' Stone is born, i.e., consciousness is created. The Philosophers' Stone is often described as the product of the *coniunctio* of sun and moon. For a man's psychology, the sun corresponds to the conscious psyche and the moon to the unconscious. Thus Jung says, "Becoming conscious of an un-

16. Marie-Louise von Franz, ed., *Aurora Consurgens*, Bollingen Series LXXVII (New York: Pantheon Books, 1966), p. 143.

conscious content amounts to its integration in the conscious psyche and is therefore a *coniunctio Solis et Lunae.*"[17]

A number of mythical and symbolic ideas can now be seen as referring to the creation of consciousness. The Gnostic idea of light scattered in the darkness requiring laborious collection is relevant, as is the grand Manichaean image of the zodiac as a vast water wheel which dips under the earth, gathers into its twelve buckets the light trapped in nature and transports it to the moon and sun.[18] The Kabbalah of Isaac Luria has profound symbolism of the same nature. According to this system, at the beginning of creation God poured His divine light into bowls or vessels, but some of the vessels could not stand the impact of the light. They broke and the light was spilled. Salvation of the world requires re-collection of the light and restitution of the broken vessels.[19]

The most outstanding symbolism pertaining to the creation of consciousness is found in alchemy. Although the texts are confused and obscure the basic idea of alchemy is quite simple. The alchemist must find the right material to start with, the *prima materia.* He must then subject it to the proper series of transformative operations in the alchemical vessel and the result will be the production of the mysterious and powerful entity called the Philosophers' Stone. We now know through Jung's profound researches that the alchemical procedure symbolizes the individuation process and that the Philosophers' Stone represents the realization of the Self, i.e., consciousness of wholeness. A crucial feature of the Philosophers' Stone is that it is a union of opposites. It is the product of a *coniunctio* often symbolized by the union of the red king and the white queen, the king and queen standing for any or all of the pairs of opposites.

17. C. G. Jung, *The Symbolic Life,* CW 18, par. 1703.
18. Hans Jonas, *The Gnostic Religion* (Boston: Beacon Press, 1958), p. 225.
19. Gershom Scholem, *Major Trends in Jewish Mysticism* (New York: Schocken Books, 1954), p. 265.

The alchemical myth tells us that consciousness is created by the union of opposites and we learn the same lesson from the dreams of individuals. For example:

> A woman dreamed that she went into an underground cavern that was divided into rooms containing stills and other mysterious-looking chemical apparatus. Two scientists were working over the final process of a prolonged series of experiments, which they hoped to bring to a successful conclusion with her help. The end product was to be in the form of golden crystals, which were to be separated from the mother liquid resulting from the many previous solutions and distillations. While the chemists worked over the vessel, the dreamer and her lover lay together in an adjoining room, their sexual embrace supplying the energy essential for the crystallization of the priceless golden substance.[20]

There is an interesting parallel to this dream in an alchemical text:

> Do ye not see that the complexion of a man is formed out of a soul and body; thus, also, must ye conjoin these, because the philosophers, when they prepared matters and conjoined spouses mutually in love with each other, behold there ascended from them a golden water.[21]

The golden crystals and the golden water can be understood as the essence of consciousness synonymous with the Self.

Contrary to the implications of the erotic imagery, the *coniunctio* of opposites is not generally a pleasant process. More often it is felt as a crucifixion. The cross represents the union of horizontal and vertical, two contrary directional movements. To be nailed to such a conflict can be a scarcely endurable agony. Augustine makes an amazingly explicit identification between the erotic *coniunctio* and Christ's crucifixion:

20. M. Esther Harding, *Psychic Energy: Its Source and Goal,* Bollingen Series X (New York: Pantheon Books, 1947), p. 450.
21. A. E. Waite, ed., *The Turba Philosophorum* (London: William Rider and Son, Ltd., 1914), Dictum 42, p 134.

> Like a bridegroom Christ went forth from his chamber, he went out with a presage of his nuptials into the field of the world.... He came to the marriage bed of the cross, and there in mounting it, he consummated his marriage ... and he joined the woman to himself forever.[22]

The union of opposites in the vessel of the ego is the essential feature of the creation of consciousness. Consciousness is the third thing that emerges out of the conflict of twoness. Out of the ego as subject versus the ego as object; out of the ego as active agent versus the ego as passive victim; out of the ego as praiseworthy and good versus the ego as damnable and bad; out of a conflict of mutually exclusive duties—out of all such paralyzing conflicts can emerge the third, transcendent condition which is a new quantum of consciousness.

This way of putting it reveals the fact that the symbolism of the Trinity refers psychologically to the creation of consciousness. Father and Son, like God and man, are opposites which collide on the cross. The Holy Spirit as the reconciling third emerges from that collision proceeding from the Father and the Son.[23] Thus the Holy Spirit (Paraclete) can only come after the death of the Son, i.e., consciousness comes as the fruit of the conflict of twoness. Therefore Christ could say,

> It is to your advantage that I go away, for if I do not go away, the Counselor (Paraclete) will not come to you; but if I go I will send him to you. And when he comes, he will convince the world of sin and of righteousness and of judgement [the opposites and their resolution]. (John 16:7-8; Revised Standard Version)

The Counselor is the Holy Spirit who will teach "all things" (John 14:26) and guide men into "all the truth" (John 16:13).

---

22. Quoted in C. G. Jung, *Mysterium Coniunctionis,* CW 14, par. 25, note 176.
23. See Jung's essay, "A Psychological Approach to the Trinity," in *Psychology and Religion,* CW 11, pars. 277-279.

Psychologically, these statements refer to the time when all individual egos will become potential vessels for the transpersonal value of consciousness. As Jung puts it,

> The future indwelling of the Holy Spirit amounts to a continuing incarnation of God. Christ, as the begotten son of God and pre-existing mediator, is a first-born and a divine paradigm which will be followed by further incarnations of the Holy Ghost in the empirical man.[24]

The biblical statements regarding the Paraclete thus anticipate the new myth which sees each individual ego as potentially a vessel to carry transpersonal consciousness. What the Lord said about Paul may eventually apply to all: "He is a chosen vessel unto me, to bear my name." (Acts 9:15; Authorized Version)

The image of the ego as a vessel leads to the important idea of being a *carrier of consciousness,* i.e., an incarnation of transpersonal meaning. Two main archetypal figures have represented this idea in world culture, namely Buddha and Christ. We are fortunate to have two such figures. With two comes the possibility of comparison and objectivity. As long as there is but one figure embodying supreme value he can only be worshipped but not understood. With the presence of two we can discover the separate third thing which they both share; understanding and greater consciousness then become possible. What Christ and Buddha have in common is the idea of being a carrier of consciousness. Characteristically, the image emerging in the West represents the standpoint of the ego and that deriving from the East speaks from the standpoint of the Self. Together, they reveal a pair of opposites. The crucified Christ and the meditating Buddha represent consciousness as agony and consciousness as tranquil bliss— total acceptance of the bondage to matter on the one hand and total transcendence of the world on the other. United they picture the two sides of the carrier of consciousness.

The idea of the individual as a vessel for consciousness

24. Jung, *Psychology and Religion,* CW 11, par. 693.

brings to mind the symbolism of the Holy Grail. As the container for Christ's blood, the Grail carries the divine essence extracted from Christ by his ultimate experience of the opposites—the *coniunctio* of crucifixion. In many respects the blood of Christ corresponds to the Holy Spirit as Paraclete.[25] Just as the Holy Spirit is to be incarnated in empirical man, so the blood of Christ is to find a containing vessel in the psyche of the individual, thereby creating for itself a Holy Grail.

On the basis of our emerging knowledge of the unconscious the traditional image of God has been enlarged. Traditionally God has been pictured as all-powerful and all-knowing. Divine Providence was seen as guiding all things according to the inscrutable but benevolent divine purpose. The extent of divine *awareness* did not receive much attention. The new myth enlarges the God-image by introducing explicitly the additional feature of the *unconsciousness of God.* His omnipotence, omniscience and divine purpose are not always *known* to Him. He needs man's capacity to know Him in order to know Himself. In one sense this indicates a renewed awareness of the reality of the less differentiated, jealous and wrathful God of the Old Testament, with whom man must remonstrate. The divine opposites that were separated by Christianity into the eternal antagonists, Christ and Satan, are now beginning to be reunited consciously in the vessel of the modern psyche.

The new myth postulates that the created universe and its most exquisite flower, man, make up a vast enterprise for the creation of consciousness; that each individual is a unique experiment in that process; and that the sum total of consciousness created by each individual in his lifetime is deposited as a permanent addition in the collective treasury of the archetypal psyche. Speaking of the psychotherapist, Jung says:

> He is not just working for this particular patient, who may be quite insignificant, but for himself as well and his own soul,

25. For further discussion of this idea, see Edward F. Edinger, *Ego and Archetype* (New York: G. P. Putnam's Sons, 1972), p. 243.

and in so doing he is perhaps laying an infinitesimal grain in the scales of humanity's soul. Small and invisible as this contribution may be, it is yet an *opus magnum.*[26]

Certain mythical images seem to suggest that accomplishments in the personal, earthly life are transferred to the divine or archetypal realm. For instance, in early Egyptian religion the dead were thought to be turned into stars or companions of the sun. James Breasted writes:

> In the splendor of the mighty heavens the Nile-dweller...saw the host of those who had preceded him; thither they had flown as birds, rising above all foes of the air, and received by Re as the companions of his celestial barque, they now swept across the sky as eternal stars.[27]

A pyramid text describes the translation of the dead king to the heavenly realm in these words:

> The king ascends to the sky among the gods dwelling in the sky....He (Re) gives thee his arm on the stairway to the sky. "He who knows his place comes," say the gods. O Pure One, assume thy throne in the barque of Re and sail thou the sky. ...Sail thou with the Imperishable stars, sail thou with the Unwearied Stars.[28]

Similar imagery occurs in Christian symbolism in which the righteous after resurrection will ascend to heaven; thus Paul writes:

> I will tell you something that has been secret: that we are not all going to die, but we shall all be changed. This will be instantaneous, in the twinkling of an eye, when the last trumpet sounds. It will sound, and the dead will be raised, imperishable, and we shall be changed as well, because our present

26. C. G. Jung, *The Practice of Psychotherapy,* CW 16, par. 449.
27. James Breasted, *A History of Egypt* (New York: Charles Scribner's Sons, 1937), p. 64.
28. James Breasted, *Development of Religion and Thought in Ancient Egypt* (New York: Harper Torch Books, 1959), p. 136.

perishable nature must put on immortality. (I Cor. 15:51-53; Jerusalem Bible)

The figure of the apocalyptic Christ makes a similar promise in Revelation:

He who is victorious—I will make him a pillar in the temple of my God; he shall never leave it. And I will write the name of my God upon him, and the name of the city of my God, that new Jerusalem which is coming down out of heaven from my God, and my own name. (Rev. 3:12; New English Bible)

Understood psychologically, these texts refer to a transfer or translation from the temporal, personal life of the ego to the eternal, archetypal realm. Presumably the essential accomplishments of egohood, its total of accumulated consciousness, is deposited by means of a final *sublimatio* in the collective, archetypal treasury of humanity. Jung seems to be saying the same thing in describing the visions he had when on the verge of death:

I had the feeling that everything was being sloughed away.... Nevertheless something remained; it was as if I now carried along with me everything I had ever experienced or done, everything that had happened around me.... I consisted of my own history, and I felt with great certainty: this is what I am.[29]

A man's dream shortly before his death presents a similar idea:

I have been set a task nearly too difficult for me. A log of hard and heavy wood lies covered in the forest. I must uncover it, saw or hew from it a circular piece, and then carve through the piece a design. The result is to be preserved at all cost, as representing something no longer recurring and in danger of being lost. At the same time a tape recording is to be made describing in detail what it is, what it represents, its whole meaning. At the end, the thing itself and the tape are to be given to the public library. Someone says that only the library

29. Jung, *Memories, Dreams, Reflections,* pp. 290-291.

will know how to prevent the tape from deteriorating within five years.[30]

The dream was accompanied by a drawing of the circular piece that looked like this:

I understand the dream as referring to the deposit of an individual's life-effort into a collective or transpersonal treasury (the library). The carved object and the tape recording can be considered equivalent since the drawing of the object looks exactly like a reel of recording tape. This would suggest that the difficult task involves the transformation of wood into word, i.e., matter into spirit.

Based on the "Communion of Saints," Catholic theology has elaborated the idea of a "treasure of merits" which have been accumulated by the lives of Christ and the saints. A Catholic theologian writes:

> If merit properly so called is not directly communicable between members of the Christian society, at least satisfaction can be transferred, almost as a man can pay a friend's debt. The infinite satisfaction of our Lord and the superabundant satisfaction of the Virgin Mary and the saints form a treasure which the Church guards and administers, drawing upon it for the payment of the debts remitted to the faithful by indulgences.[31]

This theological myth can now be understood as an early formulation, marred by concretistic misapplications (indulgences) of the historical process whereby the psychic accomplishments of individuals are transferred to the collective archetypal psyche. The new myth postulates that no authentic

---

30. Edinger, *Ego and Archetype,* pp. 218-219.
31. A. Boudinon, "Indulgences," *Encyclopedia of Religion and Ethics,* ed. James Hastings (New York: Charles Scribner's Sons, 1922), VII, pp. 253-254.

consciousness achieved by the individual is lost. Each increment augments the collective treasury. This will be the modern, more modest version of the idea of having an immortal
soul.

Milton seems to be dealing with the same idea in this
passage from *Lycidas* (lines 70-84):

> Fame is the spur that the clear spirit doth raise
> (That last infirmity of noble mind)
> To scorn delights, and live laborious days;
> But the fair guerdon when we hope to find
> And think to burst out into sudden blaze,
> Comes the blind Fury with th' abhorrèd shears
> And slits the thin-spun life. But not the praise,
> *Phoebus* repli'd, and touch't my trembling ears
> Fame is no plant that grows on mortal soil,
> Nor in the glistering foil
> Set off to th' world, nor in broad rumour lies,
> But lives and spreads aloft by those pure eyes
> And perfect witness of all-judging Jove
> As He pronounces lastly on each deed,
> Of so much fame in Heav'n expect thy meed.

"Fame" as here used by Milton corresponds to those fruits
of the ego-life which are translated to the eternal realm and
are deposited in the collective soul. Such a fame does not
"grow on mortal soil," i.e., does not depend on being known
by men, but exists in heaven, the archetypal realm. Fame of
this sort corresponds to Milton's description of a good book,
"the precious life-blood of a master spirit, imbalm'd and trea-
sur'd up on purpose to a life beyond life."[32]

The fact that our age is a time of death and rebirth for a
central myth is indicated by the dreams and upheavals from
the unconscious of many individuals. Depth psychotherapists
who work with the products of the unconscious are in a
unique position to observe the turmoil of the collective psy-

32. John Milton, "Areopagitica," *Complete Poems and Major Prose,*
ed. Merritt Y. Hughes (New York: Odyssey Press, 1957), p. 720.

che. Apocalyptic imagery is not uncommon. Here is one remarkable example of such a dream:

I am walking along what appears to be the Palisades, overlook-
ing all of New York City. I am walking with a woman who is
unknown to me personally, we are both being led by a man
who is our guide. NYC is in a rubble—the world in fact has
been destroyed as we know it. All of NYC is just one heap of
rubble, there are fires everywhere, thousands of people are
running in every direction frantically, the Hudson river has
overflowed many areas of the city, smoke is billowing up
everywhere. As far as I can see the land has been levelled. It
was twilight; fireballs were in the sky, heading for the earth. It
was the end of the world, total destruction of everything that
man and his civilization had built up.

The cause of this great destruction was a race of great giants
—giants who had come from outer space—from the far reaches
of the universe. In the middle of the rubble I could see two of
them sitting; they were casually scooping up people by the
handful and eating them. All this was done with the same
nonchalance that we have when we sit down at the table and
eat grapes by the handful. The sight was awesome. The giants
were not all the same size or quite the same structure. Our
guide explained that the giants were from different planets and
live harmoniously and peacefully together. The guide also explained that the giants landed in flying saucers (the fireballs
were other landings). In fact the earth as we know it was
conceived by this race of giants in the beginning of time as we
know it. They cultivated our civilization, like we cultivate vege-
tables in a hot house. The earth was their hot house, so to
speak, and now they have returned to reap the fruits they had
sown, but there was a special occasion for all this which I
wasn't to become aware of till later.

I was saved because I had slightly high blood pressure. If I
had normal blood pressure or if my blood pressure was too
high I would have been eaten like almost all the others. Because I have slightly high blood pressure (hypertension) I am
chosen to go through this ordeal, and if I pass the ordeal I
would become like my guide, "a saver of souls." We walked
for an extraordinary long time, witnessing all the cataclysmic
destruction. Then before me I saw a huge golden throne, it was
as brilliant as the sun, impossible to view straight on. On the

throne sat a king and his queen of the race of giants. They were the intelligences behind the destruction of our planet as I know it. There was something special or extraordinary about them which I didn't become aware of till later.

The ordeal or task I had to perform, in addition to witnessing the world's destruction, was to climb up this staircase until I was at their level—"face to face" with them. This was probably in stages. I started climbing, it was long and very difficult, my heart was pounding very hard. I felt frightened but knew I had to accomplish this task, the world and humanity were at stake. I woke up from this dream perspiring heavily.

Later I realized that the destruction of the earth by the race of giants was a *wedding feast* for the newly united king and queen, this was the special occasion and the extraordinary feeling I had about the king and queen.

Dreams of this sort will go to make up the scriptures of the new myth. This is not a personal dream and must not be interpreted personalistically. It is a collective dream expressing the state of the collective psyche. Eight days before his death, Jung spoke of having had a vision in which a large part of the world was destroyed, but, he added, "Thank God not all of it."[33] Years before he had written of the

> mood of universal destruction and renewal that has set its mark on our age. This mood makes itself felt everywhere, politically, socially, and philosophically. We are living in what the Greeks called the *kairos*—the right moment—for a "metamorphosis of the gods," of the fundamental principles and symbols.[34]

The dream I have presented portrays this mood of "universal destruction and renewal." Strikingly, it uses the same image of harvest as appears in Revelation where one angel says to another, "'Put your sickle in and reap: harvest time has come and the harvest of the earth is ripe.' Then the one sitting in the cloud set his sickle to work on the earth, and the earth's harvest was reaped." (Rev. 14:14-16; Jerusalem Bible)

What does it mean to be eaten by giants or to be harvested

33. Hannah, *Jung: His Life and Work*, p. 347.
34. Jung, *Civilization in Transition*, CW 10, par. 585.

by angels? It means that one has been swallowed up by archetypal, non-human dynamisms. The autonomous ego, whose separate stance over and against instinct and archetype is the *sine qua non* of consciousness, has fallen into a fatal identification with the archetypes. For the individual this means either psychosis or criminal psychopathy. For a society it means a structural disintegration and general collective demoralization brought about by loss of the central myth which had supported and justified the burdensome task of being human. In Yeats's words, "The best lack all conviction, while the worst/ Are full of passionate intensity." So it was in the declining days of the Roman Empire to which Revelation refers, and so it threatens to be today.

The dreamer was saved from this fate because he had "slightly high blood pressure." This was not an external fact and there were no personal associations, so we are left with general symbolism. Blood is the life-essence, but in particular it refers to the affect-life—desirousness, passion, violence. Passionate intensity is dangerous, as Yeats implies in his phrase "the blood-dimmed tide is loosed." Too high a blood pressure would perhaps indicate a greater intensity of primitive affect than can be assimilated by the ego. Such a person would be "consumed" by the primitive archetypal energies (giants) on contact with them. Normal blood pressure, on the other hand, suggests a bland lack of reaction to the abnormal times. It is "correct" for modern man to be disturbed, to have slightly high blood pressure. It indicates his inner alarm system is still intact and there is some chance for him. His anxiety will spur him to reflection and effort that may be life-saving. A complacent attitude, on the contrary, lulls one into a false sense of security so one is quite unprepared for the encounter with the activated collective unconscious (invasion of the giants).

Climbing up the staircase belongs to the alchemical symbolism of *sublimatio*. This operation involves the transfer of material from the bottom of the flask to the top through volatilization. Psychologically it refers to the process whereby personal, particular problems, conflicts and happenings are understood from a height, from a larger perspective as aspects of a greater process, under the aspect of eternity. Once the staircase has been climbed the dreamer will meet the enthroned king and queen face to face. This is a profound image of the process of encountering and enduring the union of opposites. It is a laborious task, as the dream makes clear, but it is the only way to avoid being consumed by the activated archetypes.

The opposites are initially experienced as painful and paralyzing conflicts, but enduring and working on such conflicts promote the creation of consciousness and may lead to a glimpse of the Self as a *coniunctio*. As Jung says, "All opposites are of God, therefore man must bend to this burden; and in so doing he finds that God in his 'oppositeness' has taken possession of him, incarnated himself in him. He becomes a vessel filled with divine conflict."[35] This is precisely the "divine service . . . which man can render to God"[36] and which, according to this dream, is what is required for salvation.

Another product of the *sublimatio* process has come to my attention. It is a woman's vision showing how the history of humanity might look from an immense height and distance.

> I saw the earth covered by a single great Tree whose multiple roots fed on the Inner Sun of gold, the *lumen naturae*. It was a tree whose limbs were made of light and the branches were lovingly entangled so that it made of itself a network of beauteous love.
>
> And it seemed as if it were lifting itself out of the broken seeds of many, countless egos who had now allowed the One Self to break forth. And when one beheld this, the sun and the moon and the planets turned out to be something quite, quite other than one had thought.
>
> From what I could make out, the Lord Himself was the Alchemist, and out of collective swarming and suffering, ignorance and pollution, He was "trying" the gold.[37]

35. Jung, *Psychology and Religion*, CW 11, par. 659.
36. Jung, *Memories, Dreams, Reflections*, p. 338.
37. I am indebted to A. O. Howell for permission to quote this vision.

A notable feature of the new myth is its capacity to unify the various current religions of the world. By seeing all functioning religions as living expressions of individuation symbolism, i.e., the process of creating consciousness, an authentic basis is laid for a true ecumenical attitude. The new myth will not be one more religious myth in competition with all the others for man's allegiance; rather, it will elucidate and verify every functioning religion by giving more conscious and comprehensive expression to its essential meaning. The new myth can be understood and lived within one of the great religious communities such as Catholic Christianity, Protestant Christianity, Judaism, Buddhism, etc., or in some new community yet to be created, or by individuals without specific community connections. This universal application gives it a genuine claim to the term "catholic."

For the first time in history we now have an understanding of man so comprehensive and fundamental that it can be the basis for a unification of the world—first religiously and culturally and, in time, politically. When enough individuals are carriers of the "consciousness of wholeness," the world itself will become whole.

*

In summary, I have traced the outlines of a new myth which I believe is emerging from the life and work of Jung. This myth is not a faith but an hypothesis, based on empirical data and consistent with the scientific conscience. The new myth tells us that each individual ego is a crucible for the creation of consciousness and a vessel to serve as a carrier of that consciousness, i.e., a vessel for the incarnation of the Holy Spirit.

The individual psyche is the Holy Grail, made holy by what it contains. Consciousness is a psychic substance which is produced by the experience of the opposites suffered, not blindly, but in living awareness. This experience is the *coniunctio,* the *mysterium coniunctionis* that generates the Philosophers' Stone which symbolizes consciousness. Each individual is, to a greater or lesser extent, a participant in cosmic creation, one of the buckets in the great Manichaean wheel of light, who contributes his "widow's mite" to the cumulative treasury of the archetypal psyche realized.

Every human experience, to the extent that it is lived in awareness, augments the sum total of consciousness in the universe. This fact provides the *meaning* for every experience and gives each individual a role in the on-going world-drama of creation.

The Egyptian dwarf and teacher Bes (associated with the Egyptian mother goddess), with Horus eyes.

(Bronze figure, Egypt, c. 6th century B.C.; Louvre, Paris)

# 2

# The Meaning
# of Consciousness

*... being and knowing are identical because if a
thing does not exist no one knows it, but whatever
has most being is most known.*
—Meister Eckhart

The goal of psychotherapy, indeed of all modes of psychological development, is the maximum degree of consciousness.
Consciousness and all it signifies is the ultimate value. But
what does it signify? Do we really know what we mean when
we use the word? A dictionary of philosophy gives the following definition:

**Consciousness:** (Lat. *conscire,* to know, to be cognizant of) A
designation applied to conscious mind as opposed to a supposedly unconscious or subconscious mind and to the whole do-
main of the physical and non-material. Consciousness is generally considered an indefinable term or rather a term definable
only by direct introspective appeal to conscious experiences.
The indefinability of consciousness is expressed by Sir William
Hamilton: "Consciousness cannot be defined: we may be ourselves fully aware what consciousness is, but we cannot without
confusion convey to others a definition of what we ourselves
clearly apprehend. The reason is plain: consciousness lies at
the root of all knowledge." (*Lectures on Metaphysics,* I, 191)[1]

1. Dagobert D. Runes, ed., *Dictionary of Philosophy* (New York:
Philosophical Library, 1960), p. 64.

This description tells us no more than that consciousness cannot be defined.

In *Psychological Types,* Jung says,

> By consciousness I understand the relation of psychic contents to the *ego,* in so far as this relation is perceived as such by the ego. Relations to the ego that are not perceived as such are unconscious. Consciousness is the function or activity which maintains the relation of psychic contents to the ego. Consciousness is not identical with the *psyche* because the psyche represents the totality of all psychic contents, and these are not necessarily all directly connected with the ego, i.e., related to it in such a way that they take on the quality of consciousness.[2]

This statement offers at least a beginning for a phenomenological description of the experience of consciousness; it also states explicitly the important fact that the ego is the carrier of consciousness.

We can proceed further by examining the unconscious side of the term consciousness, namely its etymology. *Conscious* derives from *con* or *cum,* meaning "with" or "together," and *scire,* "to know" or "to see." It has the same derivation as *conscience.* Thus the root meaning of both consciousness and conscience is "knowing with" or "seeing with" an "other." In contrast, the word science, which also derives from *scire,* means simple knowing, i.e., knowing without "withness." So etymology indicates that the phenomena of consciousness and conscience are somehow related and that the experience of consciousness is made up of two factors—"knowing" and "withness." In other words, consciousness is the experience of *knowing together with an other,* that is, in a setting of twoness. I shall now examine the implications of this statement.

## Knowing

One side of the phenomenon of consciousness is the act of knowing—ultimately as mysterious a mental function as the

2. C. G. Jung, *Psychological Types,* CW 6, par. 700.

closely related term, consciousness. A whole branch of philosophy, epistemology, is devoted just to the problems and limits of knowledge. My approach, however, is not philosophical but psychological-empirical, and by this method the experience of knowing can be at least descriptively elaborated.

The psychological function of knowing or seeing requires first of all that undifferentiated, diffuse experience be split into a subject and an object, the knower and the known. This primordial division of original oneness corresponds to Erich Neumann's description of the separation of the world parents. The separation of Father Sky from Mother Earth, or light from darkness, is the original cosmogonic event marking the birth of consciousness as the ability to know. As Neumann says, "This act of cognition, of conscious discrimination, sunders the world into opposites, for experience of the world is only possible through opposites."[3] The ego separates from the pleroma, the subject of knowledge is separated from the object of knowledge and the act of knowing thus becomes possible.

The original cosmogonic process of separating subject from object must be repeated with each new increment of consciousness. Each time the ego falls into an unconscious content it can become conscious of it only by an act of separation that allows the ego to *see* the emerging psychic content and thus become disidentified from it. A symbol for this process of separating subject from object, the knower from the known, is the mirror. The mirror represents the psyche's ability to perceive objectively, to be removed from the deadly grip of raw, primordial being. Schopenhauer describes it in these words:

> [It is] indeed wonderful to see, how man, besides his life in the concrete, always lives a second life in the abstract. In the former he is abandoned to all the storms of reality and to the influence of the present; he must struggle, suffer, and die like the animal. But his life in the abstract, as it stands before his

3. Erich Neumann, *The Origins and History of Consciousness* (New York: Pantheon Books, 1954), p. 104.

rational consciousness, is the calm reflection of his life in the concrete, and of the world in which he lives. . . . Here in the sphere of calm deliberation, what previously possessed him completely and moved him intensely appears to him cold, colorless, and, for the moment, foreign and strange; he is a mere spectator and observer. In respect of this withdrawal into reflection, he is like an actor who has played his part in one scene, and takes his place in the audience until he must appear again. In the audience he quietly looks on at whatever may happen, even though it be the preparation for his own death (in the play); but then he again goes on the stage, and acts and suffers as he must.[4]

The ability to turn an unconscious complex which has one by the throat into an object of knowledge is an extremely important aspect for increasing consciousness. To extend Schopenhauer's analogy, it is as though one who was fighting for his life in the arena were magically transported to the position of spectator—desperate reality becomes an image for contemplation, and the subject as "knower" is removed beyond harm.

This idea appears in the apocryphal Acts of John. At the time of the crucifixion, John could not bear to witness Jesus' suffering and fled to the Mount of Olives. There Jesus appeared to him in a vision and explained the *meaning* of the crucifixion, i.e., enabled John to contemplate it as an objective image. Although the multitude thought Jesus the man was being crucified, John was instructed to see it symbolically:

Now what those things are I signify unto thee, for I know that you will understand. Perceive thou therefore in me the praising of the Word [Logos], the piercing of the Word, the blood of the Word, the wound of the Word, the hanging up of the Word, the suffering of the Word, the nailing [fixing] of the Word, the death of the Word, and so speak I, separating off the manhood [i.e., removing personal elements]. . . .
When he had spoken unto me these things, and others which

4. Arthur Schopenhauer, *The World as Will and Representation,* trans. E. F. J. Payne (New York: Dover Publications, 1969), I, p. 85.

I know not how to say as he would have me, he was taken up,
no one of the multitudes having beheld him. And when I went
down I laughed them all to scorn . . . holding fast this one thing
in myself, that the Lord contrived all things symbolically and
by a dispensation toward men, for their conversion and salvation.[5]

Earlier, in Chapter 95 of the Acts of John, Jesus had told his
disciples: "A mirror am I to thee that perceivest me."[6] And in
Chapter 96 he says: "Behold thyself in me . . . perceive what I
do, for thine is this passion of the manhood, which I am about
to suffer."[7]

In this text, Jesus is instructing the disciples how to separate
subject from object, how to perceive experience as a mirror
that provides an image of meaning rather than as chaotic
anguish. This corresponds to active imagination or meditative
reflection which can turn an oppressive mood into an object
of knowledge by discovering the meaningful image embedded
in the mood. Jung, describing his own decisive encounter with
the unconscious, says, "To the extent that I managed to trans-
late the emotions into images—that is to say, to find the
images which were concealed in the emotions—I was inwardly
calmed and reassured."[8]

The classic mythical example of the value of separating
subject from object by the power of reflection is found in the
myth of Perseus and Medusa: to look upon Medusa directly is
to be turned into stone, i.e., she represents a psychic content
that destroys the ego; she can be overcome only by viewing
her through reflection in the mirror-shield which Athena provides for Perseus.

I consider Athena's mirror-shield ultimately to symbolize

5. M. R. James, *The Apocryphal New Testament* (London: Oxford
   University Press, 1960), p. 256.
6. Ibid., p. 253.
7. Ibid., p. 254.
8. Jung, *Memories, Dreams, Reflections* (New York: Pantheon
   Books, 1963), p. 177.

the process of human culture itself, which redeems man from the destructive Medusan horror of raw being. Language, art, drama and learning provide the Athena mirror for humanity, allowing the psyche to emerge and develop. What Shakespeare says about drama is true for all culture-forms, they hold the mirror up to nature.[9]

Schiller describes the function of art in the same way:

> [The serious purpose of genuine art] is not merely to translate the human being into a momentary dream of freedom, but actually to *make* him free. It accomplishes this by awakening a power within him, by using and developing this power to remove to a distance of objectivity the sensory world, which otherwise only weighs us down as raw material and oppresses us as a blind force.[10]

And Nietzsche expresses a similar idea when he says that "the truly serious task of art [is] to save the eye from gazing into the horrors of night and to deliver the subject by the healing balm of illusion from the spasms of the agitations of the will."[11]

Dreams and fantasy can serve the same mirror function. For example, a man in the early stages of analysis dreamed that *he looked into a mirror and was amazed to see that his face was his father's face.* This man was identified with his father and was living out his father's unhappy fate. The dream was a mirror enabling him to see that fact—to make his identification with his father an object of knowledge. Thus the subject of knowledge (the ego) became separated from the object of knowledge (identification with the father), and the dreamer took his first step out of that identification and into greater consciousness.

9. *Hamlet,* act 3, scene 2, line 25.
10. "Introductory Essay To *The Bride of Messina,"* in *Friedrich Schiller, An Anthology for Our Time,* ed. Frederich Ungar (New York: Fredrich Ungar Publishing Co., 1960), p. 168.
11. "The Birth of Tragedy," in *Basic Writings of Nietzsche,* trans. Walter Kaufmann (New York: Modern Library, 1968), p. 118.

## Being Known

To be able to climb out of the misery of raw being into the status of a knowing subject is a part of the meaning of consciousness and at times can be a salvation. The experience of being the knowing subject, however, is only one half of the process of knowledge. The other half is the experience of being the known object. The ego as knower conquers the outer or inner "other" by relegating it to the status of known object. But this is not consciousness in the full sense of "knowing with," it is only science or simple knowing. To achieve authentic consciousness the ego must also go through the experience of being the object of knowledge, with the function of the knowing subject residing in the "other."

To some extent the experience of being the known object takes place in the course of psychotherapy. The therapist often carries the projection of the "knowing other," causing the patient to feel reduced to the status of a known object. However this transference-induced condition is partial and temporary. It is also dangerous since the patient is liable to get caught in a personal dependence on the human being who "knows" him. Dependence on the therapist becomes a substitute for dependence on the inner "knowing one," i.e., the Self. In a letter written in 1915, Jung describes vividly the dangers to the patient of being known or understood by the analyst:

> Understanding is a fearfully binding power, at times a veritable murder of the soul as soon as it flattens out vitally important differences. The core of the individual is a mystery of life, which is snuffed out when it is "grasped." ... The menacing and dangerous thing about analysis is that the individual is apparently understood: the devil eats his soul away, which naked and exposed, robbed of its protecting shell, was born like a child into the light. That is the dragon, the murderer, that always threatens the newborn divine child. He must be hidden once more from the "understanding" of humanity.[12]

12. C. G. Jung, *C. G. Jung Letters,* ed. G. Adler and A. Jaffé (Princeton: Princeton University Press, 1973), vol. 1, pp. 31-32.

As Jung indicates in other sections of the same letter, the therapist's "understanding" of the patient is a necessary cautery for neurotic aspects of the personality, however it should not be applied to the healthy psyche. Thus the full experience of being the known object of an "other" knowing subject is best not projected onto a person, but rather experienced as an encounter with the inner God-image, the Self.

The archetypal image that carries the clearest symbolic expression of the ego's experience of being the known object is the image of the Eye of God. This image played a large role in Egyptian mythology. According to Rundle Clark:

> The Eye of the High God is the Great Goddess of the universe in her terrible aspect. Originally it had been sent out into the Primeval Waters by God on an errand to bring back Shu and Tefnut to their father. Thus the Eye is the daughter of the High God. When it returned, it found that it had been supplanted in the Great One's face by another—a surrogate eye—which we can interpret as the sun or moon. This was the primary cause for the wrath of the Eye and the great turning point in the development of the universe, for the Eye can never be fully or permanently appeased. The High God...turned it into a rearing cobra, which he bound around his forehead to ward off his enemies.[13]

In the dreams of a middle-aged woman, I have found an interesting parallel to the mythological equation of eye = snake. This patient was suffering from a chronic, painful physical illness, and also was suffering psychologically in the effort to understand the meaning of her ordeal. She had this dream (reported in part):

> I am talking with friends. Something we talked about caused snakes to start crawling about the room. It was as though they had been inanimate objects on the wall that had been brought to life by something I said. I wanted to kill them but a friend said I shouldn't.

13. R. T. Rundle Clark, *Myth and Symbol in Ancient Egypt* (New York: Grove Press, 1960), pp. 220-221.

The next dream, a few days later, was this: "I went to the kitchen sink to clean it up. It was actually just wet. As I looked at it, the drops of water separated. Each drop had a center in it like fish eggs or eyes. I did not throw them away."

This woman tended to take the attitude of passive victim. These dreams occurred when she was starting to experience rebellious reactions against the victim role. The dreams indicate that paying attention to the unconscious (talking about it) brought the snakes to life. Later the snakes turned into fishes' eggs or eyes. This movement is the reverse of the Egyptian myth in which the Eye of God is turned into a rearing serpent. The idea would seem to be that the emerging instinctual reactions of protest (the snakes) are actually autonomous centers of consciousness (fishes' eyes) and hence are subjects to the ego's object. In other words, the dreamer was beginning to experience herself as the object of another subject. That "other" subject (the Self) will not tolerate the meek passivity of the victim-role, and by noting the reactions of inner protest, the woman discovered the "objective subject" within, i.e., the Self.

The image of fishes' eyes comes up in alchemy as the *oculi piscium* and corresponds to the *scintillae* or multiple luminosities in the unconscious. Jung writes:

The fishes' eyes are tiny soul-sparks from which the shining figure of the filius [divine child] is put together. They correspond to the particles of light imprisoned in the dark Physis, whose reconstitution was one of the chief aims of Gnosticism and Manichaeism.[14]

The same image is discussed in his essay "On the Nature of the Psyche,"[15] where again the multiple-eye motif is equated with multiple luminosities. To be watched by strange "fishy" eyes gives one the uncanny sense of other presences. The

14. C. G. Jung, *Mysterium Coniunctionis,* CW 14, par. 46.
15. C. G. Jung, *The Structure and Dynamics of the Psyche,* CW 8, par. 394.

fishes' eyes correspond to the multiple Eye of God as described in Zechariah: "These seven are the eyes of the Lord, which range through the whole earth." (Zech. 4:10; Revised Standard Version) The major effect of such an experience is the realization that one is not alone in the psyche.

In another Egyptian text, the Eye of God says of itself, "I am the all-seeing Eye of Horus, whose appearance strikes terror, Lady of Slaughter, Mighty One of Frightfulness."[16] The experience of being a known object, being seen by the Eye of God, can be a fearsome experience because unconscious contents, as a rule, cannot stand to be observed. They react violently to being known because this destroys or relativizes the autonomy (omnipotence) they enjoy while operating unconsciously. These unconscious contents or complexes are various aspects of ego-Self identity, which is profoundly threatened by being subordinated to the status of an object known to a transcendental subject.

Jung's first childhood dream contains the image of the eye and illustrates another aspect of its phenomenology. Between the ages of three and four he dreamed:

I discovered a dark, rectangular, stone-lined hole in the ground. I had never seen it before. I ran forward curiously and peered down into it. Then I saw a stone stairway leading down. Hesitantly and fearfully, I descended. At the bottom was a doorway with a round arch, closed off by a green curtain. It was a big, heavy curtain of worked stuff like brocade, and it looked very sumptuous. Curious to see what might be hidden behind, I pushed it aside. I saw before me in the dim light a rectangular chamber about thirty feet long. The ceiling was arched and of hewn stone. The floor was laid with flagstones, and in the center a red carpet ran from the entrance to a low platform. On this platform stood a wonderfully rich golden throne. I am not certain, but perhaps a red cushion lay on the seat. It was a magnificent throne, a real king's throne in a fairy tale. Something was standing on it which I thought at first was a tree trunk twelve to fifteen feet high and about one and a

16. Clark, *Myth and Symbol,* p. 221.

half to two feet thick. It was a huge thing, reaching almost to the ceiling. But it was of a curious composition: it was made of skin and naked flesh, and on top there was something like a rounded head with no face and no hair. On the very top of the head was a single eye, gazing motionlessly upward.

It was fairly light in the room, although there were no windows and no apparent source of light. Above the head, however, was an aura of brightness. The thing did not move, yet I had the feeling that it might at any moment crawl off the throne like a worm and creep toward me. I was paralyzed with terror. At that moment I heard from outside and above me my mother's voice. She called out, "Yes, just look at him. That is the man-eater!" That intensified my terror still more, and I awoke sweating and scared to death.[17]

The phallic eye in this dream certainly fits the description of the Eye of Horus, "whose appearance strikes terror." The fact that it is called the "man-eater" corresponds to Jung's remark that understanding "eats the soul away." The eye as phallus is analogous to the eye as snake and would allude to the creative power of seeing and being seen. Similarly, in the Old Testament *to know* [YHDA] is synonymous with *to have intercourse with*.[18]

The terror caused by the eye is due to its connection with the wrath of God. An ancient Egyptian myth of the destruction of mankind illustrates how the Eye of God can function as the instrument of divine wrath:

Re, the god who created himself, was originally king over gods and men together, but mankind schemed against his sovereignty, for he began to grow old.... When he realized that mankind was plotting against him he said to his suite: Go, summon me hither my Eye, together with Shu, Tefnut, Geb, Nut and all the fathers and mothers who were with me in the Primeval Waters.... So the gods were brought together... and they said, "Speak to us that we may hear." So Re addressed

17. Jung, *Memories, Dreams, Reflections,* pp. 11-12.
18. "Now Adam knew Eve his wife, and she conceived and bore Cain...." (Gen. 4:1)

Nun (personification of the Primeval Waters): "O eldest God, in whom I myself came into being! And you, O ancient Gods! Behold mankind, who came from my Eye,[19] have been scheming against me. Tell me what you would do about it." ... Then Nun said: "O Re, my son! O God greater than he who made him and mightier than they who created him! O you that now sit upon your throne! If your Eye were turned against those who are plotting against you, how greatly would they fear you?" ... Then the others who were about him said: "Let your Eye be sent out to seize those who are plotting evil against you. ... Let it descend upon them as Hathor." So the goddess came and slew mankind in the desert.[20]

In this text, the Eye of God is the agency of a "Last Judgment." This theme is also a symbolic expression of the ego's experience of being an object of knowledge. In many religions the "judgment of the soul" is projected into the afterlife and conceived as a post-mortem experience, in which the individual is finally subject to total scrutiny and is made the object of the comprehensive knowledge of God. Depending on the outcome of this trial he will either be acquitted and sent to paradise or condemned and sentenced to hell.

The image of the "Last Judgment" can be understood psychologically as a projection into the afterlife of the ego's encounter with the Self and the archetypal experience of being the known object of a transpersonal subject; it is an awesome experience, as the myths make clear, an experience that man has understandably tried to postpone as long as possible by transferring it to the afterlife.

The theme of being looked at or made the object of knowl-

---

19. Mankind was said to come from the tears of the Eye. Cf. "birth from the eye" motif with a case reported by Esther Harding in *The Parental Image* (New York: G. P. Putnam's Sons, 1965), figs. 17, 18, 19.

20. Clark, *Myth and Symbol*, pp. 181-182. The hieroglyphic texts with interlinear translation can be found in E. A. Wallis Budge, *The Gods of the Egyptians* (New York: Dover Publications 1969), I, pp. 388 ff.

edge comes up often in dreams. For instance, a man dreamed that *news cameras were set up to photograph him but he was trying to avoid the cameras.* Like a primitive, the dreamer was afraid of the "eye" of the camera. Sometimes during a major life crisis the explicit image of the Eye of God will appear in dreams.

For instance, a young man who was going through a crucial transition leading to enlargement of consciousness had this apocalyptic dream:

> I was in a room or house that was made of adobe bricks, very earthen. The floor had a fine powder on it like a residue from dry clay. The room was gray, very little light seemed to be in the room, yet it was illuminated. I heard the pounding of the surf outside the room. This pounding became more and more intense on the walls as it grew louder and louder. The walls began to shake and rupture. Silt was in the air from the shaking walls and covering me. Cracks and splits in the walls appeared. The room felt as if it were going to collapse on top of me. I felt I would be crushed by the bricks and the flood of water. The walls were buckling, the clay bricks loosening up and crumbling in. More and more they fell around me. My life seemed to flash through my mind. I had to get out, I could not perish here, now. I was scared. I didn't know what was on the other side except I could hear the water crashing in on the walls.
>
> With all my strength I reached far up over my head and ran toward the cracking wall. I hit and pushed the wall, again and again I stepped back and hit the wall. Behind me everything was crumbling in. I was screaming, rocks and water were all about me. Again I crashed the wall and pushed as hard as I could. The wall buckled and rippled. It split, cracked and groaned. Whole sheets of bricks that were coming in on me pushed outward by the force of my throwing my whole weight into the wall. The noise was thundering. Panic had gripped me. With another thrust I felt as if all my strength would be drained, but yet again I hit the wall in what seemed like an even stronger thrust than before. The wall fell out before me, everything behind me had silenced or was gone, I didn't know. Instinctively I looked up and saw a rounded eye that had blue sky and some white clouds in it. My perspective was one of a

Dream image of the Eye of God.
(From Marion Woodman, *The Owl Was a Baker's Daughter*)

reversed telescopic field. It seemed as if as I looked up at it, it looked down at me as if I could see the eye that was looking up at it,[21] and yet it felt to be something wholly other. I was in awe, and felt deeply humbled and inexplicably human.

Another example is the dream of a middle-aged man who was going through an important psychological transition. He had developed physical symptoms which were ominously similar to those of an illness which had killed his father when he was only a few years older than the patient's present age. These symptoms threw the man into a state of acute anxiety, which was relieved in part only after thorough medical examinations proved that the symptoms had no organic basis. During his state of anxiety, he had this dream (reported in part):

> President Nixon was addressing a large group of people in a hall. I was sitting on a bench right next to his lectern. The thought crossed my mind: if I tried to kill him, no one could stop me. Two guards in uniform came past me; one turned off all the house lights. A strange orange light came up at the back wall, where a large metal screen lifted, revealing some kind of scanning device. A loud hum became audible as the scanning device screened the hall with a mysterious ray. I saw a large eye through an opening in the back wall, looking in my direction and then roving over the hall. A shot rang out. A teenage boy who had evidently planned to kill the President had shot himself. When the lights were turned on again President Nixon was kneeling in prayer.

The chief image in this dream is the numinous Eye of God. It is evident that the patient's fear of death has constellated the theme of divine judgment. The patient has a negative father complex with unconscious hostility toward father figures indicated by the death thoughts directed toward President Nixon.

---

21. Eckhart says, "The eye wherein I see God is the same eye wherein God sees me: my eye and God's eye are one eye, one vision, one knowing, one love." *Meister Eckhart,* ed. Franz Pfeiffer, trans. C. de B. Evans (London: John M. Watkins, 1956), vol. 1, p. 240.

The appearance of the Eye of God has the effect of neutraliz-
ing this complex—the adolescent commits suicide. The manifestation of the Self has dissolved an unconscious complex
and left in its wake a religious attitude—President Nixon
bending in prayer.

Another middle-aged man, also experiencing an anxiety
state, had this dream (reported in part):

> I am on a ship whose captain is an Ahab-like figure. I see a
> strange feminine being sitting on the railing of the ship. She
> touches her forehead with a wand and at the touch a third eye
> appears. The captain on seeing this miracle rushes at the
> woman. He is overpowered effortlessly and led away.

In his associations the dreamer thought of the woman with the
third eye as "a kind of angel." Ahab represented ego inflation
to him. The captain could tolerate no happenings on his ship
outside his control. Concerning the captain being led away, he
was reminded of a biblical passage referring to Christ, "When
he ascended up on high, he led captivity captive, and gave
gifts unto men." (Eph. 4:8; Authorized Version) Interestingly,
Jung has alluded to this same passage in his description of the
ego's encounter with the Self:

> When a summit of life is reached, when the bud unfolds and
> from the lesser the greater emerges, then, as Nietzsche says,
> "One becomes two," and the greater figure, which one always
> was but which remained invisible, appears to the lesser person-
> ality with the force of a revelation. He who is truly and hope-
> lessly little will always drag the revelation of the greater down
> to the level of his littleness, and will never understand that the
> day of judgment for his littleness has dawned. But the man
> who is inwardly great will know that the long expected friend
> of his soul, the immortal one, has now really come, "to lead
> captivity captive," that is, to seize hold of him by whom this
> immortal had always been confined and held prisoner, and to
> make his life flow into that greater life—a moment of deadliest
> peril.[22]

22. C. G. Jung, *The Archetypes and the Collective Unconscious,* CW
9i, par. 217.

The most striking image in the dream is the "angel's" third eye. This would correspond to the third eye of Shiva, which in Hindu mythology is said to have dangerous, destructive qualities. Concerning the three eyes of Shiva, Alain Daniélou writes:

> The three eyes of Siva represent the sun, the moon, and fire, the three sources of light that illumine the earth, the sphere of space, and the sky. The Puranas and Upanisads speak of "him whose eyes are sun, moon and fire." (*Bhasmajabala Upanisad 1*) Through his three eyes Siva can see the three forms of time, past, present, and future. (*Mahabharata 10.1251*) The three eyes are said to shine like three suns. (*Ibid. 13.846*) The frontal eye, the eye of fire, is the eye of higher perception. It looks mainly inward. When directed outward, it burns all that appears before it. It is from a glance of this third eye that Kama, the lord of lust, was burned to ashes and that the gods and all created beings are destroyed at each of the periodical destructions of the universe. (Karapatri, "Sri Siva Tattva," *Siddhanta.* II, 1941-42, 116)[23]

Shiva's third eye is similar to the Egyptian Eye of God that can be the agency of destruction. In psychological terms the Eye will be destructive of all in the ego that is not appropriately related to the Self. In other words, it will destroy inflated ego-Self identity as represented by Ahab. According to Jacob Boehme, "Divine Wisdom . . . is the union wherein God eternally sees Himself. He being that union Himself. In the Love, the Light of God, that mirror is called the Wisdom of God; but in the Wrath it is called the all-seeing Eye."[24]

If the archetypal image of the Eye of God has been activated it means that one is going through an ordeal analogous to that of Job. Jung states that Satan in the Book of Job "is

23. Alain Daniélou, *Hindu Polytheism* (New York: Pantheon Books, 1964), p. 214.
24. Jacob Boehme, *Personal Christianity, The Doctrines of Jacob Boehme,* ed. Franz Hartman (New York: Frederich Ungar Publishing Co., 1960) p. 48.

presumably one of God's eyes which 'go to and fro in the earth and walk up and down in it' (Job 1:7)."[25] Satan has been represented as a being with many eyes. There is a Tarot deck which pictures the devil as Argus with many eyes all over his body.[26] The Eye of God is thus usually experienced as that aspect of the Self which is the "adversary" of the ego— hence the sense of ordeal which usually accompanies the experience. This description applies to all four individuals whose dreams I have presented.

**Knowing With**

We have now explored the two sides of the "knowing" factor of consciousness: 1) the experience of being the knowing subject, and 2) the experience of being the known object. One could say that we begin our psychic existence in the unconscious state of known object and only laboriously, with the growth of the ego, achieve the relatively tranquil status of knowing subject. Then, if development is to proceed, the relative freedom we have won must be relinquished as the ego becomes aware that it is the object of a transpersonal subject, namely the Self. After both these experiences the way is open for the reconciling third, which I take to be the full meaning of "knowing with."

The process of knowing is a power process. To be a knower means to dominate the known object by the power of Logos. To be the known one means to be the victim of the knower. To participate in the process of knowing means to play one of these two roles or both alternately. However, the definition of consciousness as "knowing with" has a second factor: it involves not only knowing but also "withness." Withness is the dynamism of connectedness, the relationship principle. If

25. C. G. Jung, *Psychology and Religion: East and West,* CW 11, par. 579, note 3.
26. J. E. Cirlot, ed., *A Dictionary of Symbols* (New York: Philosophical Library, 1962), p. 96.

knowing is a function of Logos, withness is a function of Eros. We thus reach the unexpected discovery that the word we use for the highest value, consciousness, is in its root meaning a *coniunctio*, a union of Logos and Eros.

The experience of knowing with can be understood to mean the ability to participate in a knowing process simultaneously as subject and object, the knower and the known. This is only possible within a relationship to an object that can also be a subject. Practically, this means either a relationship with an outer other (a person) or an inner other (the Self). In reality, both are required, although one's attitude type will determine the relative importance of outer and inner factors. The extravert gives primary emphasis to the relationship with the outer expression of the Self, and the introvert gives first value to relationship with the inner manifestation of the Self.

The process of becoming conscious requires both seeing and being seen, knowing and being known. This is not hard to understand from the standpoint of the ego; but if there is to be true withness in our knowing, the same must apply to the other center of the process, namely the Self. The Self also must need to be known as well as to know. In fact, as already noted in chapter one, in *Answer to Job* Jung tells us specifically that this is the case: "Existence is only real when it is conscious to somebody. That is why the Creator needs conscious man even though, from sheer unconsciousness, he would like to prevent him from becoming conscious."[27] Because Job has seen Yahweh's amoral nature, Yahweh is obliged to change.[28] In psychological terms, because the Self has been seen by the ego, the Self's consciousness has been promoted. In this way, God—or the Self—needs man.

The pursuit of consciousness, then, does not allow one to rest in the attitude of being known and contained in God; the ego has a responsibility to the Self to be its knowing subject as well as its known object. This idea of mutual knowing be-

27. Jung, *Psychology and Religion*, CW 11, par. 575.
28. Ibid., pars. 639 ff.

tween the ego and the Self is expressed theologically by Meister Eckhart:

> It must be understood that this is all the same thing: knowing God and being known by God, and seeing God and being seen by God. We know God and see him because he makes us know and see. Even as the luminous air is not distinguishable from its luminant, for it is luminous with what illumines it, so do *we know by being known,* by his making us conscious.[29]

And again:

> God makes us to know him, and his knowing is his being, and his making me know is the same as my knowing, so his knowing is mine: just as, in the master, what he teaches is the same as, in the pupil, the thing that he is taught. And because his knowing is mine, and his knowing is his substance, and his nature and his essence, it follows that his substance and his nature and his essence are mine. And his substance, his nature and his essence being mine, therefore I am the Son of God. Behold, brethren, what manner of love God hath bestowed upon us that we should be the Sons of God![30]

In *Aion,* Jung collects examples, especially from Gnosticism, of the image of the ignorant or unconscious God and of changes that occur in the God-image in the course of cultural development. He then summarizes his conclusions:

> These utterances on the nature of the Deity express transformations of the God-image which run parallel with changes in human consciousness, though one would be at a loss to say which is the cause of the other. The God-image is not something *invented,* it is an *experience* that comes upon man spontaneously. . . . The unconscious God-image can therefore alter the state of consciousness just as the latter can modify the God-image once it has become conscious. This, obviously, has nothing to do with the "prime truth," the unknown God—at least, nothing that could be verified. Psychologically, however, the idea of God's *agnosia* [ignorance] or of the *anennoetos theos*

29. *Meister Eckhart,* ed. Pfeiffer, vol. 1, p. 31. Italics mine.
30. Ibid., p. 23.

[unconscious God], is of the utmost importance, because it identifies the Deity with the numinosity of the unconscious.[31]

The reciprocal relations between the ego and the Self—in which the Self's knowing the ego promotes ego-consciousness and the ego's knowing the Self promotes Self-consciousness—have interesting implications. Ordinarily we think that suprapersonal powers and images are projections of our own mind; but if reciprocity exists, we equally may be projections of the transpersonal other. Two dreams of Jung's bring up this idea:

> In one dream, which I had in October 1958, I caught sight from my house of two lens-shaped metallically gleaming disks, which hurtled in a narrow arc over the house and down to the lake. They were two UFOs (Unidentified Flying Objects). Then another body . . . came speeding through the air: a lens with a metallic extension which led to a box—a magic lantern. At a distance of sixty or seventy yards it stood still in the air, pointing straight at me. I awoke with a feeling of astonishment. Still half in the dream, the thought passed through my head: "We always think that the UFOs are projections of ours. Now it turns out that we are their projections. I am projected through the magic lantern as C.G. Jung. But who manipulates the apparatus?"
>
> I had dreamed once before of the problem of the self and the ego. In that earlier dream I was on a hiking trip. I was walking along a little road through a hilly landscape; the sun was shining and I had a wide view in all directions. Then I came to a small wayside chapel. The door was ajar, and I went in. To my surprise there was no image of the Virgin on the altar, and no crucifix either, but only a wonderful flower arrangement. But then I saw that on the floor in front of the altar, facing me, sat a yogi—in lotus posture, in deep meditation. When I looked at him more closely, I realized that he had my face. I started in profound fright, and awoke with the thought: "Aha, so he is the one who is meditating me. He has a dream, and I am it." I knew that when he awakened, I would no longer be.[32]

31. C. G. Jung, *Aion,* CW 9ii, par. 303.
32. Jung, *Memories, Dreams, Reflections,* p. 323.

Since the unconscious provides the material of our dream-life, the Self becomes visible to the ego by being seen in dreams. Presumably the reverse is also true. Perhaps the life dramas of the ego are the dreams of the Self. Shakespeare says, "We are such stuff as dreams are made on."[33] Whose dreams? Perhaps our conscious lives are the symbolic dramas by means of which God becomes aware of Himself. If "all the world's a stage," who is the audience? Could God be watching the acting out of His complexes in the drama of human history? According to a Gnostic myth, the cosmos (including man) was created in order to collect and retrieve the scattered particles of light which had been lost in the beginning.[34] Evidently God needs the human ego to transmit consciousness to Him.

I offer you a personal fantasy. Suppose the universe consists of an omniscient mind containing total and absolute knowledge. But it is asleep. Slowly it stirs, stretches and starts to awaken. It begins to ask questions. What am I?—but no answer comes. Then it thinks, I shall consult my fantasy, I shall do active imagination. With that, galaxies and solar systems spring into being. The fantasy focuses on earth. It becomes autonomous and life appears. Now the Divine mind wants dialogue and man emerges to answer that need. The deity is straining for Self-knowledge and the noblest representatives of mankind have the burden of that divine urgency imposed on them. Many are broken by the weight. A few survive and incorporate the fruits of their divine encounter in mighty works of religion and art and human knowledge. These then generate new ages and civilizations in the history of mankind. Slowly, as this process unfolds, God begins to learn who He is.

\*

33. *The Tempest,* act 4, scene 1, line 156.
34. Hans Jonas, *The Gnostic Religion* (Boston: The Beacon Press, 1958), pp. 222 ff.

Near the end of his life, as noted in chapter one, Jung made the statement that expresses explicitly his conclusion regarding the general purpose and meaning of human life. It is worth repeating here:

> Man's task is . . . to become conscious of the contents that press upward from the unconscious. Neither should he persist in his unconsciousness, nor remain identical with the unconscious elements in his being, thus evading his destiny, which is to create more and more consciousness. As far as we can discern, the sole purpose of human existence is to kindle a light in the darkness of mere being. It may even be assumed that just as the unconscious affects us, so the increase in our consciousness affects the unconscious.[35]

This passage distills the work of a lifetime, a life which in my opinion is the most conscious life ever lived. If we condense the statement to its essence we arrive at this: *The purpose of human life is the creation of consciousness.*

I find it profoundly significant and very moving that Jung should choose to leave us such an unequivocal answer to the universal question of the meaning of life. Jung, the man who always used such care not to go beyond the demonstrable empirical facts, the man who required knowledge rather than belief, has decided to answer the riddle of the Sphinx. We can be sure he *knows* the answer and is not just guessing.

On the collective level, consciousness is the name for a new supreme value coming to birth in modern man. The pursuit of consciousness, "con-science," unites the goals of the two previous stages of Western history, namely religion and science. Religion (meaning "linking back") has as its essential purpose the maintaining of man's connectedness with God. This corresponds to Eros, the connecting principle, and the "withness" factor of consciousness as "knowing with." Science, on the other hand, boldly gave up the connection with the other and opted instead to pursue an increase in human knowledge. If religion is Self-oriented, science is ego-oriented. Religion is

35. Jung, *Memories, Dreams, Reflections,* p. 326.

based on Eros, science on Logos. The age now dawning will provide a synthesis for this thesis and antithesis. Religion sought linkage, science sought knowledge. The new world-view will seek *linked knowledge.*

It is already widely recognized that the pursuit of scientific knowledge as the highest goal of human endeavor is puerile and inadequate to the needs of the whole man. A return to the intellectually naive standpoint of concrete religious faith is equally inappropriate to the modern mind. A genuinely new goal and purpose for human existence is required. That new goal has been found and articulated by Jung. In his words, "Man is the mirror which God holds up before him, or the sense organ with which he apprehends his being."[36]

Thus, the individual's striving for consciousness becomes the modern formulation of the venerable idea of laboring in the vineyard of the Lord, and the new answer to the age-old question of the meaning of life.

EYE OF HORUS

36. Letter, March 28, 1953. Cited by Aniela Jaffé in "Phases in Jung's Life," *Spring 1972,* p. 136.

# 3

# Depth Psychology as the New Dispensation: Reflections on Jung's *Answer to Job*

*[We] should bend to the great task of reinterpreting all the Christian traditions . . . [and since] it is a question of truths which are anchored deep in the soul . . . the solution of this task must be possible.*
−C. G. Jung, *Answer to Job.*

In the spring of 1951 at the age of seventy-five, in a sudden burst of inspiration during a febrile illness, Jung wrote "a little essay (ca. 100 typed pages)."[1] It was virtually dictated to him from the unconscious, and as soon as it was completed his illness was over.[2] In July 1951 he writes, "If there is anything like the spirit seizing one by the scruff of the neck, it was the way this book came into being."[3] Two years later he described

1. "In the spring I was plagued by my liver, had often to stay in bed and in the midst of this *misère* write a little essay (ca. 100 typed pages)." Letter of August 30, 1951. *C. G. Jung Letters,* ed. G. Adler and A. Jaffé, Bollingen Series XCV (Princeton: Princeton University Press, 1975), vol. 2, p. 21.
2. In a letter of May 1951 he says, "I have landed the great whale." Ibid., pp. 17-18.
3. Ibid., p. 20.

it in terms of a musical composition and a drama:

> The book "came to me" during the fever of an illness. It was as if accompanied by the great music of a Bach or a Handel. ...I just had the feeling of listening to a great composition, or rather of being at a concert.[4]

> The experience of the book was for me a drama that was not mine to control. I felt myself utterly the *causa ministerialis* of my book. It came upon me suddenly and unexpectedly during a feverish illness. I feel its content as the unfolding of the divine consciousness in which I participate, like it or not.[5]

In his old age, Jung remarked that he wished he could rewrite all of his books except this one. With this book he was completely satisfied.[6] He called it *Answer to Job*.

At the outset, let me state candidly my appraisal of this book. In my opinion it has the same psychic depth and import as characterize the major scriptures of the world-religions. In accordance with the modern mind, it differs from these scriptures in its modesty of expression and in the objective consciousness that illuminates it. One should not be deceived by its personal, unpretentious style. It is this very quality that demonstrates its authenticity. Although he describes the most profound encounters between the ego and the archetypal psyche, Jung never falls into an identification with the archetype. His attitude is always that of the limited human ego, it is never inflated or grandiose.

Although the style is modest, the content is of such depth as to be beyond our current power to assimilate. It lays the groundwork for a new world-view, a new myth for modern man, a new dispensation that connects man to the transpersonal psyche in a new way. In Jung's words, his insights "may well involve a tremendous change in the God-image."[7]

4. Ibid., p. 116.
5. Ibid., p. 112.
6. Marie-Louise von Franz, *C. G. Jung: His Myth in Our Time* (New York: G. P. Putnam's Sons, 1975), p. 161.
7. *Jung Letters,* vol. 2, p. 118.

*In confinio mortis* and in the evening of a long and eventful life a man will often see immense vistas of time stretching out before him. Such a man no longer lives in the everyday world and in the vicissitudes of personal relationships, but in the sight of many aeons and in the movement of ideas as they pass from century to century.[8]

In these words Jung describes John, the author of Revelation, but they apply also to Jung himself. As Jung engages himself with Job's ordeal, the centuries that separate the two men dissolve. Jung has quite literally given a definitive answer to Job's question, "Wherefore is light given to him that is in misery, and life unto the bitter in soul?" (Job 3:20; Authorized Version) This fact seems so evident to me that I do not consider it extravagant to link Jung with Job's words: "For I know that my redeemer liveth, and that he shall stand at the latter day upon the earth." (Job 19:25) These are the latter days and Jung's insight is indeed Job's redeemer.

The title of this chapter speaks of a new dispensation, but there can be no question of a new dispensation as long as one is comfortably contained in the old one. Jung writes:

> I am not . . . addressing myself to the happy possessors of faith, but to those many people for whom the light has gone out, the mystery has faded, and God is dead. For most of them there is no going back, and one does not know either whether going back is the better way. To gain an understanding of religious matters, probably all that is left us today is the psychological approach. That is why I take these thought-forms that have become historically fixed, try to melt them down again and pour them into moulds of immediate experience.[9]

The psychological approach to religious imagery is not available at any depth to one who is contained in a particular religious myth. Jung is quite explicit about this:

8. C. G. Jung, *Answer to Job* in *Psychology and Religion: West and East*, CW 11, par. 717. (Also published separately by Princeton University Press, Princeton, 1973.)

9. Ibid., par. 148.

> I do not write for believers who already possess the whole truth, rather for unbelieving but intelligent people who want to *understand* something. . . . The believer will learn nothing from my *Answer to Job* since he already has everything. I write only for unbelievers. . . . [One might inscribe inside the jacket of the book] "Nothing here for the believing Christian."[10]

Since the Judeo-Christian myth is at the foundation of the Western psyche, we are all believers to some extent, either consciously or unconsciously; that is, we all have some residual psychic containment in that myth. This means that *Answer to Job* will be a cause of offense or misunderstanding for practically everybody.

I must make a distinction here between containment and relatedness. It is, of course, possible to be related, indeed lovingly related, to a particular religion, church or religious community without being contained in it. *Containment* is an unconscious phenomenon of psychic identification. One can be contained in a religion just as one can be contained in a family or other collective group. One then has no individual, living relation to the numinous archetypes. *Relatedness* to a religion, however, means connecting with it out of one's individual numinous experience. In the latter case we have not a community of believers, but rather a community of knowers, or better, a community of individuals, each of whom is a carrier of the living experience of the Self.

Although Jung specifically states that he addresses those for whom God is dead, he also points out that the archetypal theme of the death of God is a part of the Christian myth. "Christ himself is the typical dying and self-transforming God."[11] Christ died but he was not to be found in his tomb. "Why seek ye the living among the dead? He is not here; he has risen." (Luke 24:5) Jung writes:

> The myth says he was not to be found where his body was

10. *Jung Letters,* vol. 2, p. 197.
11. Jung, "Psychology and Religion," in *Psychology and Religion,* CW 11, par. 146.

laid. "Body" means the outward, visible form, the erstwhile but ephemeral setting for the highest value. The myth further says that the value rose again in a miraculous manner, transformed. It looks like a miracle, for, when a value disappears, it always seems to be lost irretrievably. So it is quite unexpected that it should come back. The three days' descent into hell during death describes the sinking of the vanished value into the unconscious, where, by conquering the power of darkness, it establishes a new order, and then rises up to heaven again, that is, attains supreme clarity of consciousness. The fact that only a few people see the Risen One means that no small difficulties stand in the way of finding and recognizing the transformed value.[12]

In *Answer to Job* Jung submits the basic myth of the Western psyche to an intense conscious scrutiny. He accepts the imagery as psychic reality and follows the implications of the images all the way to their conclusions. This has never been done before. As Jung says,

It is altogether amazing how little most people reflect on numinous objects and attempt to come to terms with them, and how laborious such an undertaking is once we have embarked upon it. The numinosity of the object makes it difficult to handle intellectually, since our affectivity is always involved. One always participates for or against. . . .[13]

If one is a religious believer he will be afraid of acknowledging his unconscious doubt. If one has no religious beliefs he will be afraid to admit his sense of spiritual emptiness. These are the two most common sources of offense to the readers of *Answer to Job*. Either one is offended that Jung describes Yahweh so outrageously, in contradiction to the dogmatic God-image in which he believes, or one is offended that Jung takes so seriously the primitive, anthropomorphic image of God that has long since been discredited by the rational intellect. I venture to assert that every person on first

12. Ibid., par. 149.
13. Jung, *Answer to Job*, par. 735.

encounter with *Answer to Job* will be offended to some extent in either one or the other, or perhaps both, of these ways. Whoever is gravely offended will have nothing more to do with *Answer to Job,* and that is proper since one man's meat can be another man's poison. If, however, one begins to reflect on how it is that this supposedly wise and gifted man can have such strange ideas, one may be led to the discovery of the reality of the psyche. "What most people overlook or seem unable to understand," writes Jung, "is the fact that I regard the psyche as real."[14] This is the essential issue. The reality of the psyche has only been discovered in this century and very few people are yet aware of it. *Answer to Job* is written out of a profound awareness of this reality. Next to a personal analysis, the serious study of *Answer to Job* along with Jung's other writings is perhaps the best way to discover the reality of the psyche for oneself.

At the beginning of *Answer to Job* Jung says,

> I found myself obliged to deal with the whole [Job] problem, and I did so in the form of describing a personal experience, carried by subjective emotions. I deliberately chose this form because I wanted to avoid the impression that I had any idea of announcing an "eternal truth." The book does not pretend to be anything but the voice or question of one individual.[15]

The fact is that he *does* announce an eternal truth and I think he knew it. The statement is that of a very wise and canny man who knows how to approach and talk about the *numinosum. Answer to Job* is a psychological commentary on the entire Hebrew-Christian myth as it is enshrined in the Bible in both the Old and the New Testaments. The Bible contains highly numinous archetypal contents which are dangerous to approach under certain conditions. It is relatively safe only when one is functioning out of one's unique individual wholeness. This accounts for Jung's prefatory statement and for the very personal, subjective approach which he uses

14. Ibid., par. 751.
15. Ibid., Prefatory Note.

throughout *Answer to Job*. Indeed, in this book Jung gives us an example of how to deal with the activated unconscious: it must be engaged vigorously with all our powers of mind and heart.

The Bible is dangerous only for one who is aware of psychic reality. It is not dangerous for one who is embedded in a religious orthodoxy. In that case the powerful archetypal images, like wild animals, are safely caged behind the bars of the creed. The Bible is also safe when approached from a purely rational, intellectual standpoint, as do the biblical scholars. In that case it is as if one studied pictures of Africa and its wild animals. But if one is open to the unconscious and to psychic reality, then to approach the numinous contents of the Bible is like going on a real African safari and meeting the untamed powers of life face to face.

Psychologically, the danger is inflation—to be eaten up by an archetype. The best protection is to be connected with one's wholeness, most definitely including one's dark and guilty limitations. As Jung tells us, "In these circumstances it is well to remind ourselves of St. Paul and his split consciousness: on one side he felt he was the apostle directly called and enlightened by God, and, on the other side, a sinful man who could not pluck out the 'thorn in the flesh.'"[16] Marie-Louise von Franz reports that when Jung "was once asked how he could live with the knowledge he had recorded in *Answer to Job*, he replied 'I live in my deepest hell, and from there I cannot fall any further.'"[17]

The central theme of *Answer to Job*, as of the Hebrew-Christian myth, is the relationship between man and Yahweh. Jung deals with this issue in terms of psychic reality and we will be able to understand him only if we know what Yahweh is as a psychic reality. The question is: What does Yahweh mean psychologically? In a 1933 seminar Jung made these remarks:

16. Ibid., par. 758.
17. Von Franz, *C. G. Jung*, p. 174.

For the collective unconscious we could use the word God.... [But] I prefer not to use big words, I am quite satisfied with humble scientific language because it has the great advantage of bringing that whole experience into our immediate vicinity. You all know what the collective unconscious is, you have certain dreams that carry the hallmark of the collective unconscious: instead of dreaming of Aunt This or Uncle That, you dream of a lion, and then the analyst will tell you that this is a mythological motif, and you will understand that it is the collective unconscious.... This God is no longer miles of abstract space away from you in an extra-mundane sphere. This divinity is not a concept in a theological textbook, or in the Bible; it is an immediate thing, it happens in your dreams at night, it causes you to have pains in the stomach, diarrhea, constipation, a whole host of neuroses.... If you try to formulate it, to think what the unconscious is after all, you wind up by concluding that it is what the prophets were concerned with; it sounds exactly like some things in the Old Testament. There God sends plagues upon people, he burns their bones in the night, he injures their kidneys, he causes all sorts of troubles. Then you come naturally to the dilemma: Is that really God? Is God a neurosis?... Now that is a shocking dilemma, I admit, but when you think consistently and logically, you come to the conclusion that God *is* a most shocking problem. And that is the truth, God has shocked people out of their wits. Think what he did to poor old Hosea. He was a respectable man and he had to marry a prostitute. Probably he suffered from a strange kind of mother complex.[18]

Twenty-five years later, in 1958, he writes the following in an important letter to Morton Kelsey:

The absence of human morality in Yahweh is a stumbling block which cannot be overlooked, as little as the fact that Nature, i.e., God's creation, does not give us enough reason to believe it to be purposive or reasonable in the human sense. We miss reason and moral values, that is, two main characteristics of a mature human mind. It is therefore obvious that the Yahwistic image or conception of the deity is less than [that of]

18. C. G. Jung, *The Visions Seminars* (Zurich: Spring Publications, 1976), p. 391.

certain human specimens: the image of a personified brutal force and of an unethical and non-spiritual mind, yet inconsistent enough to exhibit traits of kindness and generosity besides a violent power-drive. It is the picture of a sort of nature-demon and at the same time of a primitive chieftain aggrandized to a colossal size, just the sort of conception one could expect of a more or less barbarous society—*cum grano salis.*

This image owes its existence certainly not to an invention or intellectual formulation, but rather to a spontaneous manifestation, i.e., to religious experience of men like Samuel and Job and thus it retains its validity to this day. People still ask: Is it possible that God allows such things? Even the Christian God may be asked: Why do you let your only son suffer for the imperfection of your creation? . . .

This most shocking defectuosity of the God-image ought to be explained or understood. The nearest analogy to it is our experience of the unconscious: it is a psyche whose nature can only be described by paradoxes: it is personal as well as impersonal, moral and amoral, just and unjust, ethical and unethical, of cunning intelligence and at the same time blind, immensely strong and extremely weak, etc. This is the psychic foundation which produces the raw material for our conceptual structures. The unconscious is a piece of Nature our mind cannot comprehend. It can only sketch models of a possible and partial understanding.[19]

In *Answer to Job* Jung writes,

It is only through the psyche that we can establish that God acts upon us, but we are unable to distinguish whether these actions emanate from God or from the unconscious. We cannot tell whether God and the unconscious are two different entities. Both are border-line concepts for transcendental contents. But empirically it can be established, with a sufficient degree of probability, that there is in the unconscious an archetype of wholeness. . . . Strictly speaking, the God-image does not coincide with the unconscious as such, but with . . . [this] special content of it, namely the archetype of the self.[20]

19. *Jung Letters,* vol. 2, p. 434.
20. Jung, *Answer to Job,* par. 757.

Shortly before his death in 1961, Jung was asked by an interviewer about his idea of God. He replied, "To this day God is the name by which I designate all things which cross my willful path violently and recklessly, all things which upset my subjective views, plans and intentions and change the course of my life for better or worse."[21]

Summarizing all of these quotations, we can say that Yahweh as a psychic reality is a personification of the collective unconscious especially in its aspect of center and totality, the Self. It expresses itself in dreams and fantasies of an archetypal nature; in affects, instincts and intense energy-manifestations of all kinds; in psychic and somatic symptoms; and in its specific quality of "otherness" which goes contrary to the desires and expectations of the ego. Since the phenomena of synchronicity imply a fluid boundary between inner and outer reality, the unconscious can come to us from without as well as from within. Hence Jung can say, "God is reality itself."[22]

*Answer to Job* begins with an examination of Job's encounter with Yahweh. The Book of Job can be considered as the pivot of the Old Testament. Here for the first time Yahweh engages a man as an individual rather than as the representative of Israel, the collective nation. This book thus marks the transition from collective psychology to individual psychology, from the election of a people to the election of an individual who must now encounter the *numinosum* on his own without the supporting containment of identification with a nation or a creed. Jung obviously felt that his encounter with the unconscious paralleled Job's encounter with Yahweh; thus he writes,

> The Western God-image is the valid one for me, whether I assent to it intellectually or not. I do not go in for religious philosophy, but am held in thrall, almost crushed, and defend myself as best I can.... My living thralldom ... is local, barbaric, infantile, and absymally unscientific.[23]

21. *Good Housekeeping* magazine, December 1961.
22. Jung, *Answer to Job,* par. 631.
23. *Jung Letters,* vol. 2, p. 33.

Jung was appalled by the way Yahweh treated Job, just as he must have been appalled at the torture which he, Jung, had to endure in his encounter with the unconscious. In a 1932 seminar he expresses himself vividly:

> When Yahweh was to play a particularly bad stunt on Job, he held a meeting with the devil and they discussed what they could launch on that poor fellow on earth. It is just as if men had come together to deliberate what they could do to pester and tease a dog. It was exceedingly immoral but that was not seen then, or people would not have been so naive about it.[24]

By reliving Job's experience and by bringing to it a modern consciousness, Jung has discovered an astonishing new meaning of that experience. By standing his ground and remaining true to his own conscious judgment, Job did not succumb to the moral condemnation of his "comforters" and thus "created the very obstacle that forced God to reveal his true nature."[25] Since Job did not fall victim to the proposition that all good is from God and all bad from man, he was able to *see* God and recognize his behavior to be that "of an unconscious being who cannot be judged morally. Yahweh is a *phenomenon* and, as Job says, 'not a man.'"[26] The result is that the man Job, because of his conscious awareness, is raised above Yahweh. And further:

> If Job gains knowledge of God, then God must also learn to know himself. It just could not be that Yahweh's dual nature should become public property and remain hidden from himself alone. Whoever knows God has an effect on him. The failure of the attempt to corrupt Job has changed Yahweh's nature.[27]

24. Jung, *The Visions Seminars.* Privately distributed stenographic notes (unpublished). Part VII (Autumn 1932), p. 16. This passage is not included in the two-volume edited version published by Spring Publications (above, note 18).
25. Jung, *Answer to Job,* par. 584.
26. Ibid., par. 600.
27. Ibid., par. 617.

In other words, *"The encounter with the creature changes the creator."*[28]

According to Rivkah Kluger, Jung once put it this way:

> In his great final speech God reveals himself to Job in all his frightfulness. It is as if he said to Job: "Look, that's what I am like. That is why I treated you like this." Through the suffering which he inflicted upon Job out of his own nature, God has come to this self-knowledge and admits, as it were, this knowledge of his frightfulness to Job. *And that is what redeems the man Job.* This is really the solution to the enigma of Job, that is, a true justification for Job's fate, which, without this background, would in its cruelty and injustice remain an open problem. Job appears here clearly as a sacrifice, but also as the carrier of the divine fate, and that gives meaning to his suffering and liberation to his soul.[29]

Job is a sacrifice for Yahweh's developing consciousness, "the outward occasion for an inward process of dialectic in God."[30] Here we have a truly revolutionary realization, one that will surely take centuries to pass into general awareness.

As previously mentioned, Job is the pivotal book of the Old Testament. Considered psychologically, the Old Testament as a whole represents a vast individuation process unfolding in the collective psyche. Its pivotal crisis is Job and its culmination is the mandala vision of Ezekiel. This vision is really a foundation-image of the Western psyche. How fundamental it is is indicated by the fact that Jung uses it as the basis for his most differentiated model of the Self (described in *Aion*.)[31] It is found in the first chapter of Ezekiel and reads as follows:

> As I looked, a stormwind came from the North, a huge cloud with flashing fire, from the midst of which something gleamed

---

28. Ibid., par. 686. Italics mine.
29. Rivkah Kluger, *Satan in the Old Testament* (Evanston: Northwestern University Press, 1967), p. 129.
30. Jung, *Answer to Job,* par. 587.
31. Jung, *Aion,* CW 9ii, pars. 410 ff. In a letter to James Kirsch Jung says, "The model of the self in *Aion* is based on the Ezekiel vision." *Jung Letters,* vol. 2, p. 118.

like electrum. Within it were figures resembling four living creatures that looked like this: their form was human, but each had four faces and four wings, and their legs went straight down, the soles of their feet were round. They sparkled with a gleam like burnished bronze.

Their faces were like this: each of the four had the face of a man, but on the right side was the face of a lion, and on the left side the face of an ox, and finally each had the face of an eagle. Their faces [and their wings] looked out on all their four sides; they did not turn when they moved, but each went straight forward. [Each went straight forward; wherever the spirit wished to go, there they went; they did not turn when they moved.]

Human hands were under their wings, and the wings of one touched those of another. Each had two wings spread out above so that they touched one another's while the other two wings of each covered his body. In among the living creatures something like burning coals of fire could be seen; they seemed like torches, moving to and fro among the living creatures. The fire gleamed, and from it came forth flashes of lightning.

As I looked at the living creatures, I saw wheels on the ground, one beside each of the four living creatures. The wheels had the sparkling appearance of chrysolite, and all four of them looked the same: they were constructed as though one wheel were within another.

They could move in any of the four directions they faced, without veering as they moved. The four of them had rims, and I saw that their rims were full of eyes all around. When the living creatures moved, the wheels moved with them; and when the living creatures were raised from the ground, the wheels also were raised. Wherever the spirit wished to go, there the wheels went, and they were raised together with the living creatures; for the spirit of the living creatures was in the wheels.

Over the heads of the living creatures, something like a firmament could be seen, seeming like glittering crystal, stretched straight out above their heads.

Beneath the firmament their wings were stretched out, one toward the other. [Each of them had two covering his body.] Then I heard the sound of their wings, like the roaring of mighty waters, like the voice of the Almighty. When they

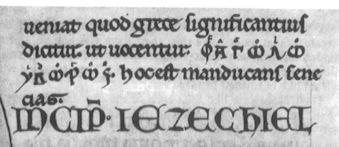

ueniat quod grece significantius
dicitur. ut uocentur: ϕ ᾶ ῒ ώ λ ώ
γ ᾶ ώ ῤ ώ ϙ· hoceft manducanf fene
aaſ

IⁿCⁱP· IEZECḢIEL

trricefimo anno inquarto menfe·ī
quinta menfiſ cum eiſem inmedio
captiuorum iuxta fluuium chobar
apti funt celi et uidi uifioneſ deꞇ·In
quinta menfiſ ipſe ē quintꝰ annuſ
tranfmigrationiſ regiſ ioachim fac
tum ē uerbum dⁿi ad hiezechielē
filium buz̧ facerdotem interra chal

The vision of Ezekiel.

(Bible of Manerius; Bibliotheque Nationale, Paris)

moved, the sound of the tumult was like the din of an army. [And when they stood still, they lowered their wings.]

Above the firmament over their heads something like a throne could be seen, looking like sapphire. Upon it was seated, up above, one who had the appearance of a man. Upward from what resembled his waist I saw what gleamed like electrum; downward from what resembled his waist I saw what looked like fire; he was surrounded with splendor. Like the bow which appears in the clouds on a rainy day was the splendor that surrounded him. Such was the vision of the likeness of the glory of the Lord. (Ezek. 1; New American Bible)

This magnificent vision is the most differentiated image of the *numinosum* to be found in the Old Testament. Earlier versions of the *numinosum*, which this vision echoes, are the pillar of cloud by day and the pillar of fire by night (Exod. 13:21); the burning bush out of which Yahweh spoke to Moses (Exod. 3:2); and the cloud that hovered over the tabernacle (Exod. 40:34).

The Ezekiel vision is a mandala, the type of symbolic image that marks the peak experience of the individuation process as it is observed in psychotherapy. We can thus consider this vision to have the same meaning in the collective individuation process of which the Old Testament is a record. It is the culmination of the Old Testament, psychologically understood, and the starting point for later Jewish mysticism[32] as well as much Cabalistic speculation. The imagery of this vision was also taken over into Christian mandalas in which the four evangelists correspond to the four creatures of Ezekiel's vision and make up the four pillars of the throne of Christ. Now depth psychology, once again, uses this great visionary image as a model for the archetype of the Self.

Yahweh suffered a moral defeat in his encounter with Job and the unnoticed result was that man was elevated above Yahweh. This required Yahweh to "catch up" with man. God

32. Gershom Scholem, *Major Trends in Jewish Mysticism* (New York: Schocken Books, 1954), p. 44.

must now become man. He must incarnate. Jung describes how the vision of Ezekiel reveals the elevation of man:

The first great vision is made up of two well-ordered compound quaternities, that is, conceptions of totality, such as we frequently observe today as spontaneous phenomena. Their *quinta essentia* is represented by a figure which has "the likeness of a human form." Here Ezekiel has seen the essential content of the unconscious, namely *the idea of the higher man* by whom Yahweh was morally defeated and who he was later to become.[33]

Ezekiel grasped, in a symbol, the fact that Yahweh was drawing closer to man. This is something which came to Job as an experience but probably did not reach his consciousness. That is to say, he did not realize that his consciousness was higher than Yahweh's, and that consequently God wants to become man. What is more, in Ezekiel we meet for the first time the title "Son of Man," which Yahweh significantly uses in addressing the prophet, presumably to indicate that he is a son of the "Man" on the throne and hence a prefiguration of the much later revelation in Christ.[34]

The term "Son of Man," which was applied to Enoch, to Ezekiel and to the Messiah, is enigmatic. Jung says this about it:

Ezekiel witnesses the humanization and differentiation of Yahweh. By being addressed as "Son of Man," it is intimated to him that Yahweh's incarnation and quaternity are, so to speak, the pleromatic model for what is going to happen, through the transformation and humanization of God, not only to God's son as foreseen from all eternity, but to man as such.[35]

This means that Ezekiel's vision, which shows God in the form of a man, indicates that Yahweh has already undergone human incarnation in the pleroma, i.e., in the unconscious. Thus henceforth, the term Son of God will be synonymous

33. Jung, *Answer to Job,* par. 665.
34. Ibid., par. 667.
35. Ibid., par. 686.

with the term Son of Man since God has become man. Mankind is now caught up in the process of divine transformation. God has fallen into man and man has become a participant in the divine drama. This fact remained on the symbolic, projected level as long as the process was confined to one man (Christ) who was worshipped as divine. But now, with the psychological understanding of this imagery, the experience becomes available potentially to all individuals.

The lowering of the relative status of Yahweh was also picked up as a major theme in Gnosticism. Ialdabaoth, the Gnostic demiurge who created the world and was equated with Yahweh, is described in Gnostic texts as ignorant and conceited. According to one text quoted by Hans Jonas, he boasted, "'I am Father and God and there is none above me,' ... to which his mother (the lower Sophia) retorts, 'Do not lie, Ialdabaoth: there is above thee, the Father of all, the First Man, and *Man* the Son of Man.'"[36] Jonas says,

> This elevation ... of "Man" to a transmundane deity, prior and superior to the creator of the universe, or, the assigning of that name to such a deity, is one of the most significant traits of gnostic theology.... It signifies a new metaphysical status of man in the order of things.[37]

We encounter the same image of a primitive, unconscious God in need of enlightenment in modern dreams. For example a woman dreamed:

> I am driving through the desert. There is a terrible, evil thing, a gorilla ape-man that is destroying people. I see some personal objects scattered about and fear that some people have had an encounter with the ape and have been destroyed. I feel safe in my car. Then I see "it" up ahead. I quickly lock the doors of my car and figure that I will drive around him and get away by sheer speed. When I see it approach rapidly and see that I cannot avoid it, I decide to crash into it and stun it

36. Irenaeus. I. 30.46. Quoted in Hans Jonas, *The Gnostic Religion,* 2nd ed. (Boston: Beacon Press, 1967), p. 134.

37. Ibid., pp. 296 ff.

and thus get away. But at the moment that we connect my car is turned all the way around and it grabs onto the car. Then something incredible happens: There is a blue light, a blue aura all around us and I hear a voice talking to me, but through a kind of mental telepathy. It is the ape talking directly to my mind. He is talking about God incarnated on earth, and about Christ and the true meaning of Christianity. The effect is as moving and powerful as I experience at times when I read the New Testament. I am amazed because I had seen "it" as the ultimate destructive force on earth and it turns out that it has some important messages. After the encounter I do not feel mortally threatened anymore. Maybe it wants to redeem me from my lowly unspiritual state—or perhaps it wants me to redeem him from the same!

This profound dream pictures the current state of the ego of Western man vis-à-vis God. We are now about to encounter the dark side of God, the *deus absconditus,* which has been left out of account in our traditional formulations. And there is the hint that, in this encounter, God will need the help of man.

A man had this dream after reading *Answer to Job:*

I see a huge ape-like man without a neck—his huge head is attached directly to his shoulders. He is naked and is looking lasciviously at a woman. I feel that he must be trained so I ask him to put on his clothes. He expels flatus loudly and leaves the room.

The dreamer associated the ape-like man to Yahweh and also to an autistic boy of his acquaintance. To connect such a dream with God is, of course, exceedingly offensive to the traditional viewpoint. And yet, this is the sort of shocking fact that we meet when we use the empirical method of exploring the psyche. As Jung says, "God *is* a most shocking problem."[38]

The idea of an unconscious God that needs man is exceedingly difficult for the traditional Western mind to accept. Even

38. Jung, *The Visions Seminars,* p. 391.

Jung's gifted pupil and colleague, Erich Neumann, was not able to accept it. In a 1959 letter to Jung he wrote, "What is creation for? The answer, that what shines only in itself when unreflected may shine in infinite variety, is age-old, but satisfies me."[39] To this Jung replied:

> Since a creation without the reflecting consciousness of man has no discernible meaning, the hypothesis of a latent meaning endows man with a cosmogonic significance, a true *raison d'être*. If on the other hand the latent meaning is attributed to the Creator as part of a conscious plan of creation, the question arises: Why should the Creator stage-manage this whole phenomenal world since he already knows what he can reflect himself in, and why should he reflect himself at all since he is already conscious of himself? Why should he create alongside his own omniscience a second, inferior consciousness—millions of dreary little mirrors when he knows in advance just what the image they reflect will look like?
>
> After thinking all this over I have come to the conclusion that being "made in the likeness" applies not only to man but also to the Creator: he resembles man or is his likeness, which is to say that he is just as unconscious as man or even more unconscious, since according to the myth of the *incarnatio* he actually felt obliged to become man and offer himself to man as a sacrifice.[40]

Another friend of Jung's provides a more painful example. Father Victor White, a Catholic priest, was unable to accept Jung's interpretation of Job. He expressed his criticism in a review of *Answer to Job,* from which I shall quote at length because it illustrates the common phenomenon of containment in a religious faith combined with a reductive-personalistic attitude toward the psyche. Father White wrote:

> Is it profitable, or even sensible, to analyse a patient's gods without analysing the patient, or without even a glance at his case history? Can it be irrelevant to all that follows that, as the

39. Quoted by Aniela Jaffé, *The Myth of Meaning* (New York: G. P. Putnam's Sons, 1971), p. 143.

40. *Jung Letters,* vol. 2, pp. 495-496.

opening verses of the Book of Job tell us, Job is materially prosperous and spiritually complacent, that he "eschews" (the Hebrew means "turns aside from," "ignores") evil, that he is driving his children to drink, that he is anxiety-ridden with the suspicion that they precisely *blaspheme,* and that he is trying to ward off this anxiety with "continual"—seemingly obsessional —ritual? Is not the subsequent "prologue in heaven" clearly a reflection of this "prologue on earth"; the God-Satan split a projection of Job's own ego-shadow split? Can we treat the archetypal antics as "autonomous," independently of Job's disturbed and anxious ego? And is it not symptomatic of the same split of ego from shadow that, as Job intensifies his repressions, his wife-anima is sick and tired of his infantile piety, his "Satan" destroys his children, produces psychosomatic boils, and drives him to withdraw from life to the dung-hill? Is not the rationalistic talk with the three "friends" typical of the agony and futility of neurotic rationalization in the presence of unconscious, existential guilt, mistaken for moral guilt? ... But most of all, I am driven to ask, what lesson, as a pupil in psychology, am I supposed to derive from it all? That we can legitimately transfer our personal splits and ills to our gods and archetypes, and put the blame on them? If so, of what greater use is psychology? Or indeed humanity's struggle for liberation from the tyranny of dark gods during the past three millenia? Or are the critics right who consider that Jungians have become so possessed by archetypes that they are in danger of abandoning elementary personal psychology altogether?[41]

This is a striking example of how talking about an archetypal image can constellate it in one's surroundings. By taking Job's side Jung has encouraged others to identify him with Job. Father White does this and then lives out the role of one of Job's "comforters" by chastising Jung. I would draw your attention in Father White's critique to the expressions, "his Satan" and "our gods and archetypes." These expressions reveal his personalistic misunderstanding of the archetypal psyche. This is inevitable in an individual for whom the archetypal psyche remains contained in a religious faith. In that case

41. *Journal of Analytical Psychology,* 4 (January 1959), pp. 77 ff.

the archetypes are understood as metaphysical entities and have not yet appeared as *psychic* reality. For such a person psychic images can have only personal reference, and religious images, at least the images of one's own religion, can have only metaphysical reference. God has not yet fallen into the psyche.

Jung replied to White's critical review in a letter. The letter is particularly gentle because Jung had just learned that Father White was suffering from an intestinal malignancy from which he died two months later at the age of fifty-eight.

Now let us assume that Job is neurotic, as one can easily make out from the textual allusions: he suffers from a regrettable lack of insight into his own dissociation. He undergoes an analysis of a sort, f.i. by following Elihu's wise counsel; what he will hear and what he will be aware of are the discarded contents of his personal subconscious mind, of his shadow, but not the divine voice, as Elihu intends. You faintly insinuate that I am committing Elihu's error too, in appealing to archetypes first and omitting the shadow. *One cannot avoid the shadow* unless one remains neurotic, and as long as one is neurotic one has omitted the shadow. The shadow is the block which separates us most effectively from the divine voice. Therefore Elihu in spite of his fundamental truth belongs to those foolish Jungians, who, as you suggest, avoid the shadow and make for the archetypes, i.e., the "divine equivalents," which by the way are nothing but escape camouflage according to the personalistic theory.

If Job succeeds in swallowing his shadow he will be deeply ashamed of the things which happened. He will see that he has only to accuse himself, for it is his complacency, his righteousness, his literal-mindedness, etc. which have brought all the evil down upon him. He has not seen his own shortcomings but has accused God. He will certainly fall into an abyss of despair and inferiority feeling, followed, if he survives, by profound repentance. He will even doubt his mental sanity: that he, by his vanity, has caused such an emotional turmoil, even a delusion of divine interference—obviously a case of megalomania.

After such an analysis he will be less inclined than ever before [to think] that he has heard the voice of God. Or has

Freud with all his experience ever reached such a conclusion? If Job is to be considered as a neurotic and interpreted from the personalistic point of view, then he will end where psychoanalysis ends, viz. in disillusionment and resignation, where its creator most emphatically ended too.

Since I thought this outcome a bit unsatisfactory and also empirically not quite justifiable, I have suggested the hypothesis of archetypes as an answer to the problem raised by the shadow.[42]

Jung here expresses the crux of the matter. If the psychic images that express the *numinosum*—the supreme meaning and value of the psyche—are understood personalistically and reductively, the soul is destroyed and one is left with only disillusionment, resignation and despair. If, however, like Job, one does not succumb to the personalistic-reductive interpretation of his inner agony—an interpretation that tells him it is all his own fault—he may, like Job, be granted an experience of the *numinosum.* And that experience brings with it an awareness that the ego has a *reason* to exist, that it is needed for the *realization* of the Self.

The personalistic-reductive attitude belongs to a naive, uninitiated, ego-centered consciousness that knows no other psychic center but its own. Jung says:

All modern people feel alone in the world of the psyche because they assume that there is nothing there that they have not made up. This is the very best demonstration of our God-almighty-ness, which simply comes from the fact that we think we have invented everything psychical—that nothing would be done if we did not do it; for that is our basic idea and it is an extraordinary assumption.... Then one is all alone in one's psyche, exactly like the Creator before the creation. But through a certain training...something suddenly happens which one has not created, something objective, and then one is no longer alone. That is the object of [certain] initiations, to train people to experience something which is not their inten-

---

42. *Jung Letters,* vol. 2, p. 545. For a more candid comment see *Quadrant,* 8 (Winter 1975), pp. 17 ff.

tion, something strange, something objective with which they cannot identify. . . .

This experience of the objective fact is all-important, because it denotes the presence of something which is not I, yet is still psychical. Such an experience can reach a climax where it becomes an experience of God.[43]

Job did not take personal blame or responsibility for his woes, but rather insisted that he was not the creator of everything that happened to him. Psychologically, this would correspond to an ego-attitude which does not identify with the phenomena of the objective psyche. Jung was once asked why patients chose to have certain psychological symptoms. He protested vigorously, saying that was like asking a man who had been devoured by a crocodile why he chose that particular one to eat him.[44] When one has discovered the reality of the psyche he is spared such mistakes. Likewise, he will not subscribe to the dictum, "all good from God, all bad from man." As Jung says, this leads to "the absurd result that the creature is placed in opposition to its creator and a positively cosmic or daemonic grandeur in evil is imputed to man. . . . [which] burdens him with the dark side of God."[45] In other words, man becomes God's scapegoat.

Hints of this realization are to be found in the Bible. For instance in Psalm 51, the *Miserere,* which refers to David's guilt after being with Bathsheba, we read,

> Have mercy on me, O God, in your goodness,
> in your great tenderness wipe away my faults;
> wash me clean of my guilt,
> purify me from my sin.
> For I am well aware of my faults,
> I have my sin constantly in mind,
> having sinned against none other than you,

43. Jung, *The Visions Seminars,* p. 73.
44. Richard Evans, *Conversations with Carl Jung,* Insight Book (Princeton: D. Van Nostrands, 1964), p. 106.
45. Jung, *Answer to Job,* par. 739.

having done what you regard as wrong.
That you may be found just when you pass sentence
 on me,
blameless when you give judgement.
               (Pss. 51:1-4; Jerusalem Bible alt. rdg.)

In this passage, the astonishing realization is dawning that God is justified by man. Speaking in psychological terms, the ego takes responsibility for the evil promptings of the Self in order that it (the Self) may be transformed.

A similar idea was expressed by Omar Khayyam in the eleventh century:

> Oh Thou, who didst with pitfall and with gin
> Beset the Road I was to wander in,
>    Thou wilt not with Predestined Evil round
> Enmesh, and then impute my Fall to Sin!
>
> Oh Thou, who Man of baser Earth didst make,
> And e'en with Paradise devise the Snake:
>    For all the Sin wherewith the Face of Man
> Is blacken'd—Man's forgiveness give—and take![46]

Another aspect of Jung's revolutionary realization is his interpretation of the myth of incarnation. Since Yahweh had suffered a moral defeat by Job, man was elevated above God and God must therefore become that superior creature, man. In Jung's words, "the immediate cause of the incarnation lies in Job's elevation, and its purpose is the differentiation of Yahweh's consciousness."[47] This differentation is evidenced by the complete *separatio* that Yahweh undergoes with the advent of Christ. His two sides represented by his good son, Christ, and his evil son, Satan, are totally separated, indeed dissociated, from each other. Christ becomes identical with Yahweh through the doctrine of the *homoousia,* while Satan is cast out of heaven and thus condemned to live the life of a dissociated, autonomous complex.

46. *The Rubaiyat of Omar Khayyam,* ed. Edward Fitzgerald, verses 80-81.

47. Jung, *Answer to Job,* par. 642.

Herein lies the reason for Jung's observation that Yahweh's incarnation in Christ is incomplete. It left out of account Yahweh's dark side. This is reflected in the myth of the immaculate conception and the everlasting virginity of Mary. Jung writes:

> Her freedom from original sin sets Mary apart from mankind in general, whose common characteristic is original sin and therefore the need for redemption. The *status ante lapsum* is tantamount to a paradisal, i.e., pleromatic and divine, existence. By having these special measures applied to her, Mary is elevated to the status of a goddess and consequently loses something of her humanity: she will not conceive her child in sin, like all other mothers, and therefore he also will never be a human being, but a god. To my knowledge at least, no one has ever perceived that this queers the pitch for a genuine Incarnation of God, or rather, that the Incarnation was only partially consummated. Both mother and son are not real human beings at all, but gods.[48]

> [The incarnation was incomplete.] If it had been complete, the logical consequence, the *parousia,* would have taken place. But Christ was in error about it.[49]

The incomplete incarnation of Yahweh in Christ leads Jung to the idea of the continuing incarnation. This is already suggested by the Apostle Paul:

> Everyone moved by the Spirit is a son of God. The spirit you received is not the spirit of slaves bringing fear into your lives again; it is the spirit of sons, and it makes us cry out, "Abba, Father." The Spirit himself and our spirit bear united witness that we are children of God. And if we are children we are heirs as well: heirs of God and coheirs with Christ, sharing his sufferings so as to share his glory. (Rom. 8:14-17; Jerusalem Bible)

The Gospel of John also implies a continuing incarnation. Christ says that when he leaves he will send the Paraclete.

48. Ibid., par. 626.
49. *Jung Letters,* vol. 2, p. 156.

(John 16:7) "The Advocate, the Holy Spirit, whom the Father will send in my name, will teach you everything and remind you of all I have said to you." (John 14:26) After citing these texts Jung says,

> The continuing direct operation of the Holy Ghost on those who are called to be God's children implies, in fact, a broadening process of incarnation. Christ, the son begotten by God, is the first-born who is succeeded by an ever-increasing number of younger brothers and sisters.[50]

From this viewpoint the imitation of Christ takes on a new meaning. Christ's precepts as outer rules of behavior are no longer to be taken literally and concretely. Rather, one is to live his own reality as totally as Christ lived his. To the extent that one lives in conscious relation to the Self he will experience Christ as his brother since Christ is our outstanding example of such a life.

> It is not an "imitation of Christ" but its exact opposite: an assimilation of the Christ-image to his own self....It is no longer an effort, an intentional striving after imitation, but rather an involuntary experience of the reality represented by the sacred legend.[51]

In psychological terms, the incarnation of God means individuation. To the extent that one becomes aware of the transpersonal center of the psyche, the Self, and lives out of that awareness, one can be said to be incarnating the God-image. This experience involves encounter with the opposites. The Self is a union of opposites. When it first emerges into consciousness the opposites split apart and the ego is faced with the conflict of their opposition. Jung says:

> All opposites are of God, therefore man must bend to this burden; and in so doing he finds that God in his "oppositeness" has taken possession of him, incarnated himself in him. He becomes a vessel filled with divine conflict.[52]

50. Jung, *Answer to Job,* par. 658.
51. C. G. Jung, *Mysterium Coniunctionis,* CW 14, par. 492.
52. Ibid., par. 659.

God acts out of the unconscious of man and forces him to harmonize and unite the opposing influences to which his mind is exposed from the unconscious.[53]

The hallmark of individuation is the differentiation of the individual psyche from its containment in the collective psyche. This process is accompanied by a progressive awareness of the transpersonal psyche and the task of mediating and humanizing its energies. "As soon as a more honest and more complete consciousness beyond the collective level has been established," writes Jung, "man is no more an end in himself, but becomes an instrument of God, and this is *really* so."[54]

The individuating ego is commandeered by the transpersonal psyche (God, Self) and drafted like Job into the service of making it more conscious. The ego is confronted with non-personal images and non-personal energies and its task will be to relate to these images and energies. The images require to be understood and the energies as affects require containment and humanization. These images and affects can quite properly be called Yahweh-images and Yahweh-affects. They are expressions of the original, unconscious Self and, lacking any understanding of them by the ego, they are indistinguishable from so-called narcissism and infantile omnipotence. They are manifestations of ego-Self identity.[55] Jung refers to this when he says,

We don't know... how much of God... has been transformed. ...It can be expected that we are going to contact spheres of a not yet transformed God when our consciousness begins to extend into the sphere of the unconscious.[56]

Once a conscious ego has established itself vis-à-vis the transpersonal images and energies, it is no longer appropriate

53. Ibid., par. 740.
54. *Jung Letters,* vol. 2, p. 242.
55. For a further discussion of this idea see Edward F. Edinger, *Ego and Archetype* (Baltimore: Penguin Books, 1973), chapter 1.
56. *Jung Letters,* vol. 2, p. 314.

to use the reductive terminology of the infantile and the narcissistic. Now the appropriate terms will be found in the new myth of the continuing incarnation of God. As the ego wrestles with the transpersonal energies to humanize them, it will be reliving Jacob's encounter with the angel and Job's encounter with Yahweh. And like Job, we can expect to find within our antagonist, the unconscious, also our redeemer. When the unconscious buffets us most severely with storms of affect or depression, we can also expect to find in dreams and fantasy the healing meaning that rescues.

God has fallen out of containment in religion and into the unconscious of man, i.e., he is incarnating. Our unconscious is in an uproar with the God who wants to know and to be known.[57] Jung writes:

> The unconscious wants to flow into consciousness in order to reach the light,[58] but at the same time it continually thwarts itself, because it would rather remain unconscious. That is to say, God wants to become man, but not quite.[59]

A modern dream that refers to the incarnation of Yahweh is relevant here. A man dreamed that *he saw a primitive sorcerer holding up an animal skin. A living face was visible on the skin. It was a kind of oracle.* The dreamer immediately associated the primitive sorcerer to Yahweh. The animal skin reminded him of the fact that certain early manuscripts of the Bible were written on vellum. He associated the face to the image of Christ's face on Veronica's veil. He was also reminded of a flayed human skin with a face in Michelangelo's great mural of the Last Judgment in the Sistine Chapel. The face on the flayed skin is a self-portrait of Michelangelo, who

---

57. See above, chapter 2.
58. This will often be experienced by the conscious ego very much the way the world of light experienced invasion by the world of darkness in the Gnostic myth. See Jonas, *The Gnostic Religion*, pp. 213 ff.
59. Jung, *Answer to Job*, par. 740.

pictures himself as the flayed skin of St. Bartholomew, the Christian martyr who was flayed alive.

This dream tells us that the primitive sorcerer, Yahweh, manifests through the animal skin containing the human face, i.e., he manifests through man. The events of the Bible are the evidence of Yahweh written in the history of human beings, just as his incarnation in Christ gave us a glimpse of his living face. In addition, the association to the face and flayed skin of Michelangelo suggests that the creative artist is a manifestation of the deity. Michelangelo's self-portrait indicates that he was identified with Marsyas, the musician in Greek mythology who challenged Apollo to a musical contest and when he lost was flayed alive. The myth of Marsyas applies to some extent to every creative artist, and it is also a feature of individuation inasmuch as acknowledging and living out of a connection with the Self does involve a Marsyas-like presumption followed by torments.

Flaying symbolizes a transformation process which on the one hand lays bare the inner man, and on the other hand signifies the extraction of the soul (skin = soul).[60] A sonnet of Michelangelo's refers to the theme of flaying:

> To others merciful and only to
> Itself unkind, this lowly creature who
> Sloughs off its skin in pain that it may give
> Pleasure to others, dies that they may live.
>
> So do I long for such a destiny—
> That from my death, my Lord, you might alone
> Take life, then by my death I too might be
> Changed like the worm which casts its skin on
> stone.
>
> For if that skin were mine I could at least
> Be woven in a gown to clasp that breast,
> And so embrace the beauty which I crave.

60. Jung, "Transformation Symbolism in the Mass," *Psychology and Religion*, CW 11, par. 348; see also Jung, *Alchemical Studies*, CW 13, par. 95 and note 116.

> Then would I gladly die. Or could I save
> My Lord's feet from the rain by being shoes
> Upon his feet—this also would I choose.[61]

The idea of being shoes for God is an explicit incarnation image. Michelangelo is here giving expression to the most profound meaning of the flaying motif. The words he wrote concerning Dante apply equally to him: "He did not fear to plumb the places where/Failure alone survives."[62]

Returning to the dream, it seems to be saying that Yahweh manifests himself on man's skin; that is where he incarnates. Job belongs alongside of Christ, Marsyas and Michelangelo in this respect. Job got "skinned" by Yahweh and we are granted a picture of Yahweh's face via the "skin" of Job who risked his skin to contend with God like Marsyas. This image is relevant to everyone who submits himself to the process of individuation. He will be offering up his "skin" to be a kind of vellum manuscript upon which Yahweh writes his revelation.

\*

At the beginning of the present era, the Jewish religion with its rich and profound tradition of man's encounter with Yahweh was recast and reinterpreted in the light of the new divine revelation in Christ. Man was thought to have a new relation to God, signified by a new covenant and a new dispensation. The Latin word *dispensatio* was used to render the Greek *oikonomia,* which means literally administration of a household. The usage is illustrated in Ephesians where Paul says,

> To me, the least of all the saints, is given this grace, to preach among the Gentiles, the unsearchable riches of Christ, and to enlighten all men, that they may see what is the dispensation of the mystery which hath been hidden from eternity in God. (Eph. 3:8-9; Douay Version)

61. *The Sonnets of Michelangelo,* trans. Elizabeth Jennings (New York: Doubleday & Co., 1970), Sonnett XXI, p. 52.
62. Ibid., Sonnet II, p. 32.

The significant phrase is "dispensation of the mystery," *oikonomia tou mysteriou*. It is as though man's relation to the hidden mystery of God must be dispensed or administered much as the economy of a household is administered. In psychological terms it means, I think, the provision of a world-view that relates man (ego) to God (archetypal psyche) and promotes the smooth transfer of energy from one realm to the other.

The transition from one dispensation to another is demonstrated in the Letter to the Hebrews which was once attributed to Paul. The author states that the Jewish priesthood has been superseded by the eternal priesthood of Christ; the sacrificial offerings of the priests have been replaced by Christ's sacrifice of himself, and the temple sanctuary has been replaced by a heavenly sanctuary "not made by hands." Sacrifices no longer need be repeated. Christ's sacrifice has occurred once and for all and one need only have faith in him to be redeemed. The author writes:

> Now Christ has come, as the high priest of all the blessings which were to come. He has passed through the greater, the more perfect tent, which is better than the one made by men's hands because it is not of this created order; and he has entered the sanctuary once and for all, taking with him not the blood of goats and bull calves, but his own blood, having won an eternal redemption for us. The blood of goats and bulls and the ashes of a heifer are sprinkled on those who have incurred defilement and they restore the holiness of their outward lives; how much more effectively the blood of Christ who offered himself as the perfect sacrifice to God through the eternal Spirit can purify our inner self from dead actions so that we do our service to the living God. (Heb. 9:11-14; Jerusalem Bible)

This passage describes a process of transition from a literal sacrificial ritual to one more spiritualized and abstract. It is a step toward the psychological realization of service to the Self, but it concretizes the symbolic image of Christ and projects onto him the sacrificial function. The experience of the Self thus remains collectivized and contained within the *participation mystique* of a religious community, although it will be none the less real for that.

The Christian dispensation brought about a new *oikonomia* to administer man's relation to the divine. That mode of administration is now largely exhausted, and, if my perception is accurate, a new mode is on the horizon, namely depth psychology. *The new psychological dispensation finds man's relation to God in the individual's relation to the unconscious.* This is the new context, the new vessel with which humanity can be the carrier of divine meaning.

In essence, the Jewish dispensation was centered in the *law,* the Christian dispensation was centered in *faith* and the psychological dispensation is centered in *experience.* God is now to be carried experientially by the individual. This is what is meant by the continuing incarnation. Jung puts it this way in an important letter to Elined Kotschnig:

> Although the divine incarnation is a cosmic and absolute event, it only manifests empirically in those relatively few individuals capable of enough consciousness to make ethical decisions, i.e., to decide for the Good. Therefore God can be called good only inasmuch as He is able to manifest His goodness in individuals. His moral quality depends upon individuals. That is why He incarnates. Individuation and individual existence are indispensable for the transformation of God the Creator.[63]

If the individual stands over against the primitive Yahweh-affects within him; if he allows them to live without repressing them and without identifying with them; if he struggles to extract the images of meaning that lie embedded in them; if he patiently and diligently seeks the way of individuation which the unconscious both reveals and withholds—then his efforts will have a gradual transformative effect on Yahweh. He will be offering himself as a crucible for the transformation of the dark God and contributing his widow's mite to the cosmic drama of continuing creation.

63. *Jung Letters,* vol. 2, p. 314.

# 4

# The Transformation
# of God

*We all must do just what Christ did. We
must make our experiment.*
—C.G. Jung, *C.G. Jung Speaking.*

To those unacquainted with Jung's empirical psychological
method this chapter may be open to misunderstanding. It may
sound like theology, but it is not. It is, in fact, empirical
psychology. The confusion comes in the use of terms which
have traditional religious connotations. Why then use these
terms? It is necessary to do so in order to demonstrate the
psychological facts which underlie religious conceptions;
moreover, there is scarcely any other way to communicate
such material.

The objective psyche was first experienced and described in
a religious, metaphysical context, hence traditional religious
images are our richest source of data concerning the objective
psyche. Depth psychology, however, melts down the dogmatic
structures which were the traditional containers of these images and recasts them in modern molds of understanding.
According to the psychological standpoint man cannot get
outside his own psyche. All experience is therefore psychic
experience. This means that it is impossible, experientially, to
distinguish between God and the God-image in the psyche.
My use of the term "God" in this chapter, therefore, always
refers to the God-image in the psyche, i.e., the Self.

On June 30, 1956, Jung wrote the remarkable letter referred
to at the end of chapter three, in which he speaks of the

continuing incarnation and the transformation of God. Elined Kotschnig had asked him "for an answer to the problem of an unconscious, ignorant creator-god and if this did not imply 'some principle, some Ground of Being, beyond such a demiurge.'"[1] Jung's reply, written in English, is a most profound document which deserves our closest scrutiny. In that letter Jung writes, speaking of Christ:

> He was up against an unpredictable and lawless God who would need a most drastic sacrifice to appease His wrath, viz. the slaughter of His own son. Curiously enough, as on the one hand his self-sacrifice means admission of the Father's amoral nature, he taught on the other hand a new image of God, namely that of a Loving Father in whom there is no darkness. This enormous antinomy needs some explanation. It needed the assertion that he was the Son of the Father, i.e., the incarnation of the Deity in man. As a consequence the sacrifice was a self-destruction of the amoral God, incarnated in a mortal body. Thus the sacrifice takes on the aspect of a highly moral deed, of a self-punishment, as it were.
>
> Inasmuch as Christ is understood to be the second Person of the Trinity, the self-sacrifice is the evidence for God's goodness. At least so far as human beings are concerned. We don't know whether there are other inhabited worlds where the same divine evolution also has taken place. It is thinkable that there are many inhabited worlds in different stages of development where God has not yet undergone the transformation through incarnation. However that may be, for us earthly beings the incarnation has taken place and we have become participants in the divine nature and presumably heirs of the tendency towards goodness and at the same time subject to the inevitable self-punishment. As Job was not a mere spectator of divine unconsciousness but fell a victim to this momentous manifestation, in the case of incarnation we also become involved in the consequences of this transformation. Inasmuch as God proves His goodness through self-sacrifice He is incarnated, but in

---

1. *C. G. Jung Letters,* ed. G. Adler and Aniela Jaffé, Bollingen Series XCV (Princeton: Princeton University Press, 1975), vol. 2, p. 312, note 1.

view of His infinity and the presumably different stages of cosmic development we don't know of, how much of God—if this is not too human an argument—has been transformed? In this case it can be expected that we are going to contact spheres of a not yet transformed God when our consciousness begins to extend into the sphere of the unconscious. There is at all events a definite expectation of this kind expressed in the "Evangelium Aeternum" of the Revelations containing the message: Fear God! (Rev. 14:6-7)

Although the divine incarnation is a cosmic and absolute event, it only manifests empirically in those relatively few individuals capable of enough consciousness to make ethical decisions, i.e., to decide for the Good. Therefore God can be called good only inasmuch as He is able to manifest His goodness in individuals. His moral quality depends upon individuals. That is why He incarnates. Individuation and individual existence are indispensable for the transformation of God the Creator.[2]

In this passage Jung gives a psychological interpretation of the Christian myth and explains how that myth applies to modern man. However, the statement is so condensed that it requires both commentary and amplification to make it generally accessible. I would draw your attention particularly to the statement, "it can be expected that we are going to contact spheres of a not yet transformed God when our consciousness begins to extend into the sphere of the unconscious." This remark is the source of the title for this chapter.

As Jung demonstrates in *Answer to Job*, Yahweh is an unpredictable and lawless God who often falls into fits of rage and jealousy. The Old Testament documents this fact thoroughly and it is demonstrated empirically to anyone who has an encounter in depth with the objective psyche. According to the symbolism of the Christian myth, Christ's sacrifice changed the nature of Yahweh. By offering himself as an object upon which the divine wrath can vent itself, Christ proclaims a benevolent God of love and brings redemption to man from the wrathful God. Like a heroic soldier who throws

2. Ibid., pp. 313-314.

himself upon a live grenade and thereby rescues his company at the cost of his own life, so Christ allows himself to be blasted by the wrath of God in order to redeem his fellow men. This sacrificial act not only redeems man but also transforms Yahweh. With his explosive rage spent by the innocent victim's voluntary acceptance of it, Yahweh is transformed into a God of love through the example of a loving man.

The situation is complicated by the fact that Christ is not only a man but also is considered to be the son of God. Thus Christ's self-sacrifice is simultaneously God's sacrifice of himself, or, as Jung says, "a self-destruction of the amoral God, incarnated in a mortal body." It seems as though God can undergo transformation only by being incarnated in man. He needs a mirror of himself in mortal form to bring the consciousness required for change. And what mortal can serve that mighty aim but one who perceives himself as a son of God, i.e., an agent of divinity? In other words, the ego is given the strength and purpose to stand against the primitive Self through awareness of its sonship with the Self, which confers a sense of partnership in the mutual process of transformation.

The theme of the transformation of God did not first appear with the advent of Christ. As Jung has pointed out in *Answer to Job,* Job's encounter with Yahweh brought about such a transformation.[3] The Old Testament also provides us with other examples of the transformation of God through his encounter with conscious man. In Genesis Yahweh is contemplating the destruction of Sodom and Gomorrah. Abraham exhorts God to be just, in these words:

> "Are you really going to destroy the just man with the sinner? Perhaps there are fifty just men in the town. Will you really overwhelm them, will you not spare the place for the fifty just men in it? Do not think of doing such a thing: to kill the just man with the sinner, treating just and sinner alike! Do not think of it! Will the judge of the whole earth not administer

---

3. C. G. Jung, *Psychology and Religion: West and East,* CW 11, par. 640.

justice?" Yahweh replied, "If at Sodom I find fifty just men in
the town, I will spare the whole place because of them."

Abraham replied, "I am bold indeed to speak like this to my
Lord, I who am dust and ashes. But perhaps the fifty just men
lack five: will you destroy the whole city for five?" "No," he
replied, "I will not destroy it if I find forty-five just men
there." Again Abraham said to him, "Perhaps there will only
be forty there." "I will not do it," he replied, "for the sake of
the forty."

Abraham said, "I trust my Lord will not be angry, but give
me leave to speak: perhaps there will only be thirty there." "I
will not do it," he replied, "if I find thirty there." He said, "I
am bold indeed to speak like this, but perhaps there will only
be twenty there." "I will not destroy it," he replied, "for the
sake of the twenty." He said, "I trust my Lord will not be
angry if I speak once more: perhaps there will only be ten." "I
will not destroy it," he replied, "for the sake of the ten." (Gen.
18:23-32; Jerusalem Bible)

As a result of this encounter, a righteous remnant, Lot and his
family, are rescued from the doomed city of Sodom.

In Numbers Yahweh is enraged at the rebellion of the
Israelites and threatens to destroy the entire nation by pesti-
lence. Moses remonstrates successfully, as follows:

"But the Egyptians already know that you, by your own power,
have brought this people out from their midst. They have said
as much to the inhabitants of this country. They already know
that you, Yahweh, are in the midst of this people, and that you
show yourself to them face to face; that it is you, Yahweh,
whose cloud stands over them, that you go before them in a
pillar of cloud by day and a pillar of fire by night. If you
destroy this people now as if it were one man, then the nations
who have heard about you will say, 'Yahweh was not able to
bring this people into the land he swore to give them, and so
he has slaughtered them in the wilderness.' No, my Lord! It is
now you must display your power, according to those words
you spoke, 'Yahweh is slow to anger and rich in graciousness,
forgiving faults and transgression, and yet letting nothing go
unchecked, punishing the father's fault in the sons to the third
and fourth generation.' In the abundance, then, of your graciousness, forgive the sin of this people, as you have done from

Egypt until now." Yahweh said, "I forgive them as you ask."(Num. 14:13-20; Jerusalem Bible)

Most instructive of all is the mysterious account of the sacrifice of Isaac, also referred to as the *Akedah* or binding of Isaac:

It happened some time later that God put Abraham to the test. "Abraham, Abraham," he called. "Here I am," he replied. "Take your son," God said, "your only child Isaac, whom you love, and go to the land of Moriah. There you shall offer him as a burnt offering, on a mountain I will point out to you."

Rising early next morning Abraham saddled his ass and took with him two of his servants and his son Isaac. He chopped wood for the burnt offering and started on his journey to the place God had pointed out to him. On the third day Abraham looked up and saw the place in the distance. Then Abraham said to his servants, "Stay here with the donkey. The boy and I will go over there; we will worship and come back to you."

Abraham took the wood for the burnt offering, loaded it on Isaac, and carried in his own hands the fire and the knife. Then the two of them set out together. Isaac spoke to his father Abraham, "Father," he said. "Yes, my son," he replied. "Look," he said, "Here are the fire and the wood, but where is the lamb for the burnt offering?" Abraham answered, "My son, God himself will provide the lamb for the burnt offering." Then the two of them went on together.

When they arrived at the place God had pointed out to him, Abraham built an altar there, and arranged the wood. Then he bound his son Isaac and put him on the altar on top of the wood. Abraham stretched out his hand and seized the knife to kill his son.

But the angel of Yahweh called to him from heaven. "Abraham, Abraham," he said. "I am here," he replied. "Do not raise your hand against the boy," the angel said. "Do not harm him, for now I know you fear God. You have not refused me your son, your only son." Then looking up, Abraham saw a ram caught by its horns in a bush. Abraham took the ram and offered it as a burnt offering in place of his son. (Gen. 22:1-14; Jerusalem Bible)

Embedded in this text I see a symbolic description of the process of the transformation of God. The clue to this interpretation is the fact that the divine name changes in the course of the account. At the beginning, the divine name is "*Elohim*," i.e., God. At the end of the story, when Abraham is restrained from sacrificing Isaac, the name used is Yahweh. From the standpoint of Biblical criticism, this means that two different documents (the E and J documents) have been combined to make the canonical text. However, from the standpoint of empirical psychology, which reads the dream or scripture as it stands, it means that a transformation of the deity has occurred. The same thing is indicated by the fact that God has changed his mind and no longer wants Isaac to be sacrificed.

The text begins with the statement that God "put Abraham to the test." What is the nature of that test? Abraham was caught between two different levels of divine manifestation—a primitive God (*Elohim*) requiring human sacrifice, and a more differentiated and merciful God (Yahweh). One biblical scholar notes:

> In Abraham's day the sacrifice of the firstborn was a common practice among the Semitic races, and was regarded as the most pleasing service which men could offer to their deities. It was the "giving of their firstborn for their transgression, the first of their body for the sin of their soul." (Mic. 6:7)[4]

Abraham is in the fearful position of having to mediate between two developmental levels of deity. That is his test.

The primitive level of deity is represented by the ram, which according to legend was grazing in Paradise before it was transported to the thicket on Mount Moriah.[5] The ram signifies unregenerate archetypal energy which must be extracted from the unconscious and sacrificed. Abraham is participating in a process of divine transformation by permitting himself to entertain murderous impulses against Isaac. This

4. J. R. Dummelow, *The One Volume Bible Commentary* (New York: Macmillan Publishing Co., 1973), p. 22.
5. Erich Wellisch, *Isaac and Oedipus* (London: Routledge & Kegan Paul, 1954), p. 70.

brings the ram-energy into consciousness where it can then be sacrificed under the aegis of the more differentiated aspect of God. Psychologically one might say that Abraham's test determined whether he was willing to risk a conscious encounter with his primitive affects in the faith that they are capable of transformation.

The Church Fathers considered Isaac to be a prefiguration of Christ. For instance, Augustine says that Isaac "himself carried to the place of sacrifice the wood on which he was to be offered up, just as the Lord himself carried His own cross." Also the ram "caught by the horns in the thicket: What then did he represent but Jesus, who, before He was offered up, was crowned with thorns by the Jews?"[6] According to this association, Yahweh's test of Abraham is to determine whether Abraham is willing to share Yahweh's later ordeal of sacrificing his son, Christ. Abraham is asked to participate in the tragic drama of divine transformation. He assents, allowing it to be said of Abraham as well as of Yahweh that he "loved...so much that he gave his only son." (John 3:16; Jerusalem Bible)

Before leaving Old Testament imagery I want to draw your attention to a remarkable passage in Ezekiel. Yahweh is speaking. He has been complaining to Ezekiel about the sins of Israel and threatening to destroy the nation in punishment. Then he says:

> I have been looking for someone among them to build a wall and man the breach in front of me, to defend the country and prevent me from destroying it; but I have not found anyone. Hence I have discharged my anger on them; I have destroyed them in the fire of my fury. (Ezek. 22:30-31; Jerusalem Bible)

From this we learn that Yahweh actively seeks a man who will stand up to his attack and defend the breach in the defensive boundaries of the ego. Yahweh is asking to be resisted in his wrathful, destructive side in order that his primitive aspect can undergo transformation. Martin Luther quotes

6. Augustine, *City of God,* XVI, 32.

this passage from Ezekiel and adds that the strong hedge (or wall) is "the upright prayer of a godly Christian."[7] In psychological language this means that active imagination by an ego which is related to the Self will help to transform the primitive affects of the primordial psyche.

Certain figures in Greek mythology are also victims of the drama of divine transformation. Robert Graves gives us an example in the following account of the myth of Tantalus:

Tantalus was the intimate friend of Zeus, who admitted him to Olympian banquets of nectar and ambrosia until, good fortune turning his head, he betrayed Zeus's secrets and stole the divine food to share among his friends. Before this crime could be discovered, he committed a worse. Having called the Olympians to a banquet on Mount Sipylus, or it may have been at Corinth, Tantalus found that the food in his larder was insufficient for the company and, either to test Zeus's omniscience, or merely to demonstrate his good will, cut up his son Pelops, and added the pieces to the stew prepared for them, as the sons of Lycaon had done with their brother Nyctimus when they entertained Zeus in Arcadia. None of the gods failed to notice what was on their trenchers, or to recoil in horror, except Demeter who, being dazed by her loss of Persephone, ate the flesh from the left shoulder.

For these two crimes Tantalus was punished with the ruin of his kingdom and, after his death by Zeus's own hand, with eternal torment in the company of Ixion, Sisyphus, Tityus, the Danaids, and others. Now he hangs, perennially consumed by thirst and hunger, from the bough of a fruit-tree which leans over a marshy lake. Its waves lap against his waist, and sometimes reach his chin, yet whenever he bends down to drink, they slip away, and nothing remains but the black mud at his feet; or, if he ever succeeds in scooping up a handful of water, it slips through his fingers before he can do more than wet his cracked lips, leaving him thirstier than ever. The tree is laden with pears, shining apples, sweet figs, ripe olives and pomegranates, which dangle against his shoulders; but whenever he

7. *The Table Talk of Martin Luther,* ed. Thomas S. Kepler (Grand Rapids: Baker Book House, 1979), p. 205.

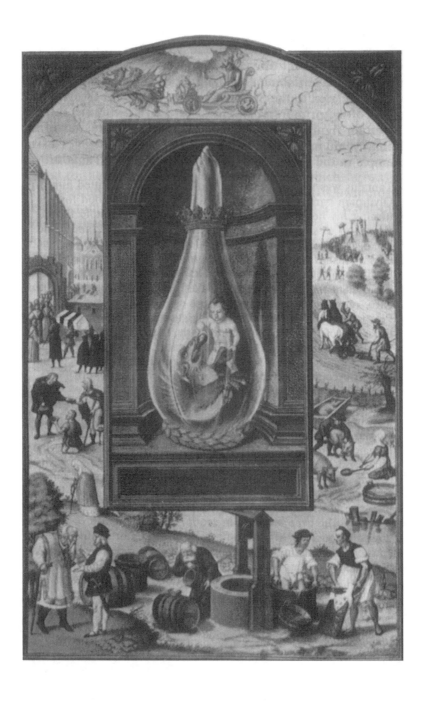

reaches for the luscious fruit, a gust of wind whirls them out of his reach.

Moreover, an enormous stone, a crag from Mount Sipylus, overhangs the tree and eternally threatens to crush Tantalus's skull.[8]

Tantalus was admitted into fellowship with the Gods, i.e., he represents an ego which has made intimate contact with the transpersonal psyche and has become privy to the secrets beyond the "epistemological curtain." This makes him a participant in the drama of divine transformation. Like Isaac, he is caught between two successive stages in the evolution of God. Zeus is in a state of transition out of cannibalism. Reading between the lines of the myth which comes down to us in a late recension, we can make out the outlines of a primitive deity who requires human sacrifice and whose food is human flesh. The flesh of Pelops serves as divine ambrosia! A symbolic parallel is the flesh of Christ which constitutes the Eucharistic feast of the Mass.

Tantalus, having feasted with the gods, knows their secret menu and offers it to them. The gods, perceiving their cannibalistic shadow in the mirror of their human counterpart, recoil in horror and project their newly-perceived shadow onto Tantalus. Tantalus thus becomes the scapegoat of the gods, an instrument for the increase of divine consciousness, at the cost of his own torment.

The punishment of Tantalus is to be perpetually tantalized. His desire is forever excited and forever denied. This image of simultaneous arousal and frustration has a precise parallel in alchemy. In *Splendor Solis* by Solomon Trismosin, the stages of the transformation process are depicted in a series of seven pictures representing the sealed and crowned *vas hermetis*. The first picture (opposite) shows a sealed vessel within which is a fiery dragon tended by a naked child or homunculus. In the child's right hand is a bottle from which he is pouring water

8. Robert Graves, *The Greek Myths* (New York: George Braziller, Inc., 1957), vol. 2, pp. 25-26.

down the dragon's throat. In his left hand is a bellows with which he is fanning the flame. The text speaks of opening the holes and cracks of the earth "to receive the influence of Fire and Water."[9] The picture illustrates the operation of the opposites, fire and water being applied simultaneously. This is exactly what happens to Tantalus; his desire is simultaneously inflamed and extinguished. The primitive, desirous aspect of the transpersonal psyche collides with the spiritual principle of restraint and self-denial, and Tantalus becomes a living crucible for the transformation of God.

Another example is Sisyphus, who name means "the very wise one" or perhaps "divinely wise."[10] His story is as follows: One day Zeus abducted Aegina, daughter of the river god Asopus. He took her to the isle of Oenone where he raped her. Sisyphus happened to witness this event and he gave the information to Asopus in return for a spring of fresh water, the Peirene spring. For revealing divine secrets,

> Sisyphus was given an exemplary punishment. The Judges of the Dead showed him a huge block of stone—identical in size with that into which Zeus had turned himself when fleeing from Asopus—and ordered him to roll it up the brow of a hill and topple it down the farther slope. He has never yet succeeded in doing so. As soon as he has almost reached the summit, he is forced back by the weight of the shameless stone, which bounces to the very bottom once more; where he wearily retrieves it and must begin all over again, though sweat bathes his limbs, and a cloud of dust rises above his head.[11]

It is Sisyphus's knowledge of the nature of Zeus that harnesses him to his perpetual burden. The account I have quoted explicitly identifies the stone of Sisyphus with Zeus.

9. Solomon Trismosin, *Splendor Solis* (1582) (London: Kegan Paul, Tench, Trubner & Co., Ltd. rpt.; n.d.), p. 34 and plate XII.

10. Jane Harrison, *Prolegomena to the Study of Greek Religion,* 3rd ed. (Cambridge: Cambridge University Press, 1922), p. 608.

11. Graves, *Greek Myths,* vol. 1, p. 218.

The same conclusion can be extracted from another tradition. According to Robert Graves,

> Sisyphus's "shameless stone" was originally a sun-disk, and the hill up which he rolled it is the vault of heaven; this made a familiar enough icon. The existence of a Corinthian Sun cult is well established: Helios and Aphrodite are said to have held the acropolis in succession, and shared a temple there (Pausanias: ii 4.7). Moreover, Sisyphus is invariably placed next to Ixion in Tartarus, and Ixion's fire-wheel is a symbol of the sun.[12]

Zeus and Helios are alternative images for deity. In either case, mortal Sisyphus is burdened with a task beyond his power to consummate. Because he has seen God, Sisyphus becomes a carrier of the divine burden. He saw Zeus as kidnapper and rapist, and it was this insight into divine darkness that imposed the intolerable burden upon him. Sisyphus's consciousness of God had the effect of an incarnation. As mover of the sun, Sisyphus shares the task of the creator in bringing forth the light. God is incarnated in Sisyphus, who in the midst of his torture participates in the transformation of God. He enhances the light (rolls the sun disk) by carrying awareness of the darkness of God.

The transformation of God is also the secret and essential meaning of alchemy. The *prima materia* which was to be transformed into the Philosophers' Stone by the alchemical process was sometimes identified explicitly with God.[13] An occasional text even draws a parallel between the alchemical transformation and the passion of Christ, as in this outstanding example:

> And firstly it is here to be noted, that the Sages have called this decomposed product, on account of its blackness (Cant. 1), the raven's head. In the same way Christ (Isa. 53) had no form nor comeliness, was the vilest of all men, full of griefs and

12. Ibid., p. 219.
13. C. G. Jung, *Psychology and Alchemy*, CW 12, par. 431; see also Jung, *The Practice of Psychotherapy*, CW 16, par. 533, note 24.

sicknesses, and so despised that men even hid their faces from him, and he was esteemed as nothing. Yea, in the 22nd Psalm [Vulgate] he complains of this, that he is a worm and no man, the laughing-stock and contempt of the people; indeed, it is not unfitly compared with Christ when the putrefied body of the Sun lies dead, inactive, like ashes, in the bottom of the phial, until, as a result of greater heat, its soul by degrees and little by little descends to it again, and once more infuses, moistens, and saturates the decaying and all but dead body, and preserves it from total destruction. So also did it happen to Christ himself, when at the Mount of Olives, and on the cross, he was roasted by the fire of the divine wrath (Matt. 26, 27), and complained that he was utterly deserted by his heavenly Father, yet none the less was always (as is wont to happen also to an earthly body through assiduous care and nourishing) comforted and strengthened (Matt. 4, Luke 22) and, so to speak, imbued, nourished, and supported with divine nectar; yea, when at last, in his most sacred passion, and at the hour of death, his strength and his very spirit were completely withdrawn from him, and he went down to the lowest and deepest parts below the earth (Acts 1, Eph. 1, I Peter 3), yet even there he was preserved, refreshed, and by the power of the eternal Godhead raised up again, quickened, and glorified (Rom. 14), when finally his spirit, with its body dead in the sepulchre, obtained a perfect and indissoluble union, through his most joyful resurrection and victorious ascension into heaven, as Lord and Christ (Matt. 28) and was exalted (Mark 16) to the right hand of his Father; with whom through the power and virtue of the Holy Spirit as true God and man he reigns and rules over all things in equal power and glory (Ps. 8), and by his most powerful word preserveth and upholdeth all things (Hebr. 1) and maketh all things one (Acts 17). And this wondrous Union and divine Exaltation angels and men, in heaven and on earth and under the earth (Philipp. 2, I Peter 1) can scarce comprehend, far less meditate upon, without fear and terror; and his virtue, power, and roseate Tincture is able even now to change, and tint, and yet more, perfectly to cure and heal us sinful men in body and soul: of which things we shall have more to say below... Thus, then, we have briefly and simply considered the unique heavenly foundation and corner-stone Jesus Christ, that is to say, *how he is compared and united with the earthly philosophical stone of the Sages, whose material and preparation, as we have heard, is an outstanding type and lifelike image of the incarnation of Christ.* [14]

Note that this text equates the creation of the Philosophers' Stone with the incarnation of God in Christ. From here it is but a step to the equation of individuation with divine incarnation. The passage quoted links the alchemical procedure with the torturous ordeal of Christ. We have already noted that Tantalus and Sisyphus endured torture as a consequence of their knowledge of deity. Another example of the connection between torture and transformation is found in the *Visions of Zosimos,* a work of early Greek alchemy discussed by Jung. In these visions the alchemical transformation process is pictured as human torture. In a dream Zosimos encounters a figure who speaks to him as follows:

"I am Ion, the priest of the inner sanctuaries, and I submit myself to an unendurable torment. For there came one in haste at early morning, who overpowered me, and pierced me through with the sword, and dismembered me in accordance with the rule of harmony. And he drew off the skin of my head with the sword, which he wielded with strength, and mingled the bones with the pieces of flesh, and caused them to be burned on the fire of the art, till I perceived by the transformation of the body that I had become spirit. And that is my unendurable torment." And even as he spoke thus, and I held him by force to converse with me, his eyes became as blood. And he spewed forth all his own flesh. And I saw how he changed into the opposite of himself, into a mutilated anthroparion, and he tore his flesh with his own teeth, and sank into himself. [15]

Other images in the text include boilings, burnings and dismemberments for the purpose of turning "body into spirit" and to "make the eyes clairvoyant and raise the dead." I refer to this grisly text because it is an alchemical parallel to the

---

14. Quoted in C. G. Jung, *Mysterium Coniunctionis,* CW 14, par. 485.

15. Quoted in C. G. Jung, *Alchemical Studies,* CW 13, par. 86.

tortured figures of Greek myth, and also because Jung gives us an explicit comment on the meaning of Zosimos's torture dreams:

> The drama shows how the divine process of change manifests itself to our human understanding and how man experiences it —as punishment, torment, death, and transfiguration. The dreamer describes how a man would act and what he would have to suffer if he were drawn into the cycle of the death and rebirth of the gods, and what effect the *deus absconditus* would have if a mortal man should succeed by his "art" in setting free "the guardian of the spirits" from his dark dwelling.[16]

Jung was such a mortal man who succeeded by his art in setting free the guardian of the spirits from his dark dwelling and he suffered the torture of that accomplishment. As previously noted, when Jung was once asked "how he could live with the knowledge he had recorded in *Answer to Job,* he replied 'I live in my deepest hell, and from there I cannot fall any further.'"[17]

A dream has come to my attention that is relevant to our theme. It was dreamt by a woman who was later to become a Jungian analyst:

> A young boy is in his father's laboratory stealing secrets. He is quiet and deadly serious. The laboratory is in semidarkness, but the boy knows where to go to get what he wants. The father discovers the boy and punishes him by burying him alive. The father then sits beside the grave and awaits the time when the boy can be let out of his earth-grave. (This takes place on a kind of dark lunar landscape.) The father will only allow himself to be seen from the back. One cannot look at the face of the father.
>
> The son is then exhumed and sits in a semidark room at a desk. He has dark circles under his eyes and his young face is worn and tired, far beyond his years. The father and son are

16. Ibid., par. 139.

17. Marie-Louise von Franz, *C. G. Jung: His Myth in Our Time* (New York: G. P. Putnam's Sons, 1975), p. 174.

strangely connected. It is as if this drama of stealing and burial has occurred many, many times. It seems to be as hard on the father as it is on the son. Each knows that it will occur again. Each has to endure it.

This dream is an interesting combination of the themes of Prometheus, Christ and modern science. Like Prometheus, the son in the dream is stealing secrets from the father; like Christ, he is punished by burial and then resurrected; and like a modern scientist his theft of Nature's secrets takes place in a laboratory, i.e., by means of the empirical attitude.

The image of Prometheus stealing the divine fire for the benefit of man, then enduring the eternal punishment of being chained to a rock and having his liver fed upon daily by the eagle of Zeus, is central to the enterprise of Western consciousness. Like Tantalus and Sisyphus, Prometheus came into possession of divine secrets. Unlike Tantalus and Sisyphus, Prometheus's acquisition of secret knowledge was deliberate, and signifies the willful ego's striving for consciousness.

At the time of the genesis of the Prometheus myth—perhaps four thousand years ago—taking on the divine burden was conceived as a crime against God. Now, today, it becomes possible for modern man to open himself to the divine influx for the purpose of serving God rather than stealing from him. Thus Jung writes in a letter:

Can man stand a further increase of consciousness? . . . Is it really worthwhile that man should progress morally and intellectually? Is that gain worth the candle? That's the question. . . . I confess that I submitted to the divine power of this apparently unsurmountable problem and I consciously and intentionally made my life miserable, because I wanted God to be alive and free from the suffering man has put on him by loving his own reason more than God's secret intentions.[18]

This statement of Jung's would correspond to Prometheus deciding to steal fire from Zeus not for the benefit of man,

18. Quoted in Gerhard Adler, "Aspects of Jung's Personality and Work," *Psychological Perspectives,* 6 (Spring 1975), p. 12.

but because Zeus was suffering from the burdensome weight of too much fire and needed human assistance to carry the tormenting load. In fact this *is* Jung's vision of the nature of things. As he says in the letter to Elined Kotschnig, "It can be expected that we are going to contact spheres of a not yet transformed God when our consciousness begins to extend into the sphere of the unconscious."[19] And, since it is man's task to become more and more conscious,[20] he is therefore drafted into participation in the divine drama of God's transformation.

The dream concerns the theme of God's transformation. Father and son refer to God and man or Self and ego. The father's laboratory is the world, within and without—the world as nature and the world as history. The son is human consciousness carried by the individual ego who must make the world an object of knowledge, i.e., steal divine secrets. There is punishment, i.e., pain, accompanying this action.

The image of burial in the earth is reminiscent of the Gnostic myth of Sophia's descent into matter whereby light penetrates the darkness. It is a *coagulatio* symbol[21] which alludes to the process of incarnation. The transpersonal, archetypal factor takes on earthiness and is entombed in flesh, i.e., manifests in an individual ego. Just as Prometheus is fixed to the earth by being chained to the rock, so the son in the dream is buried in the earth. Experientially this refers to the fact that each new conscious insight carries with it a new

19. *Jung Letters,* vol. 2, p. 314.
20. "Man's task is . . . to become conscious of the contents that press upward from the unconscious. Neither should he persist in his unconsciousness, nor remain identical with the unconscious elements of his being, thus evading his destiny, which is to create more and more consciousness." C. G. Jung, *Memories, Dreams, Reflections* (New York: Pantheon Books, 1963), p. 326.
21. Edward F. Edinger, "Psychotherapy and Alchemy IV: *Coagulatio,*" *Quadrant,* 12 (Summer 1979), p 25.

responsibility which weighs one down. Awareness is depressing, it buries one in the earth. Nietzsche expresses this fact in his poem, "Between Birds of Prey":

> Encaved within thyself,
> Burrowing into thyself,
> Heavy-handed,
> Stiff,
> A corpse—
> Piled with a hundred burdens,
> Loaded to death with thyself,
> A knower!
> Self-knower! The wise Zarathustra!
> You sought the heaviest burden
> And found yourself.[22]

As Jung says, the "heavy burden the hero carries is *himself,* or rather *the* self, his wholeness, which is both God and animal—not merely the empirical man, but the totality of his being, which is rooted in his animal nature and reaches out beyond the merely human towards the divine."[23]

Thus, in the above dream, after each theft of a secret (increase of consciousness), the son is buried in the earth (weighed down with the burden of responsibility that the new consciousness imposes). The dream states that this is a necessary and repeated process. Father and son are parts of a perpetual, cyclic drama of theft, burial and resurrection. The purpose of this sequence is the progressive transfer and realization of latent consciousness and responsibility from the father to the son, which is equivalent to the incarnation of God in the human ego. Motivated by the autonomous urge to individuation (the Holy Ghost), the ego must strive to know the Self and to realize it consciously. As Jung says, "[Individuation]... means practically that he [man] becomes adult,

22. Quoted in C. G. Jung, *Symbols of Transformation,* CW 5, par. 459.
23. Ibid., par. 460.

responsible for his existence, knowing that he does not only depend on God but that God also depends on man."[24]

In the Book of Job Yahweh says, "Behold now behemoth ... he is the chief of the ways of God." (Job 40:15, 19; Authorized Version). And again, "Canst thou draw out leviathan with an hook? ... Shall the companions make a banquet of him?" (Job 41:1, 6). Behemoth and Leviathan represent the primordial psyche, what Jung calls "the not yet transformed God." According to Jewish legend, the flesh of Behemoth and Leviathan will be served at the messianic banquet. A midrash says,

> In that hour the Holy One, blessed be He, will set out tables and slaughter Behemoth and Leviathan ... and prepare a great banquet for the pious. ... And the Holy One, blessed be He, will bring them wine that was preserved in its grapes since the six days of creation. ... And he brings all the fine things of the Garden of Eden.[25]

The messianic age signifies psychologically the coming of the Self, the achievement of individuation. As the legend puts it, the primordial psyche becomes food for the pious. In other words, it will be transformed and humanized as it is *assimilated* by the ego under the guidance of the Self.

Another image of the mastering of Leviathan is found in certain medieval representations picturing Christ on the cross as the bait of God's fishing line which catches Leviathan (opposite).[26] This is another symbol of the "pious" ego which, like Christ, willingly exposes itself to the primordial psyche for the purpose of transforming it. Such an ego is undergoing individuation and is an example of continuing incarnation.

Another dream relevant to our subject is that of a woman painter who was in the process of committing herself to her artistic vocation:

24. *Jung Letters,* vol. 2, p. 316.
25. Raphael Patai, *The Messiah Texts* (New York: Avon Books, 1979), pp. 238-239.
26. Jung, *Psychology and Alchemy,* CW 12, fig. 28.

I am with a few people and we are suddenly startled to see a gigantic bird overhead. His wingspread is enormous—twenty to thirty feet. As he swoops down low we are in his awesome shadow. This bird has numbers on his wing, and I know that he belongs to a man who will be very distressed that he has flown away. We must capture him and return him to the man. The bird lands on the ground—not afraid of us. One man picks up his hind hoof and begins tapping the dirt out of it (the way one does to a horse). This hoof is no ordinary hoof, it is inlaid with jewels; that is why it is being cleaned. Later a freight train comes by and we are able to load the huge bird aboard the train for his trip home. We have sedated him to make the trip easier, and he is carefully secured.

The imagery in this dream is related to Gabriel's Annunciation to the Virgin Mary. "The Holy Ghost shall come upon thee, and the power of the Highest shall overshadow thee: therefore also that holy thing which shall be born of thee shall be called the Son of God." (Luke 1:35; Authorized Version) The great bird is clearly the Holy Ghost manifested as the dreamer's creative genius. The dreamer is overshadowed by the awesome bird just as Mary is overshadowed by the "power of the Highest." The dream has some interesting variations from the biblical Annunciation. In contrast to the angel Gabriel, the bird is lost and its owner (presumably God) is distressed by its absence. Under the circumstances, human help is needed to capture the bird and to transport it back to its home.

This dream has a collective as well as a personal significance. The Holy Ghost, the autonomous transpersonal spirit that connects man with God, has been lost by modern man. Like the Gnostic Sophia, it has fallen into the darkness of matter. This explains the image of the great bird in need of help. Like a member of an endangered species, it must be caught, restrained, sedated and transported to a more favorable habitat. Asleep and constrained within mortal flesh, the Holy Spirit is being carried to its goal. The dream reverses the usual imagery in which the autonomous spirit is the active guide and inspiration of man. It plays a modern variation on the traditional theme. The Holy Spirit, which has lost its sacred connotations during its descent into matter, must now be rescued by the conscious ego and restored to its rightful connection with God.

A later dream by the same woman reveals yet another side of the incarnation phenomenon:

> I am standing with a man outdoors in a city. From a construction site a few blocks away we suddenly hear an enormous explosion. A huge, black metal ring is thrust up into the sky by the blast and then comes hurtling back down. It is so large that I know its impact wherever it lands will kill many people. We hear the terrible crash and I cry as I feel this sudden tragedy.

This also can be seen as a collective dream. The explosive emergence of the great black ring represents a collective phenomenon we are currently witnessing, namely, the birth of the dark Self out of the earthly efforts of man. Ours is a time of great promise and great peril. As the dream indicates, proximity to such an explosive event is dangerous. One may be crushed under the wheel of the juggernaut. The danger is greater the more psychologically naive one is. For us an adequate knowledge of the psyche is probably a matter of life and death. If the emergent God that wants to be born in man is not humanized and transformed by a sufficient number of conscious individuals, its dark aspect can destroy us.

As it gradually dawns on people, one by one, that the transformation of God is not just an interesting idea but is a living reality, it may begin to function as a new myth. Whoever recognizes this myth as his own personal reality will put his life in the service of this process. Such an individual offers himself as a vessel for the incarnation of deity and thereby promotes the on-going transformation of God by giving Him human manifestation. Such an individual will experience his life as meaningful and will be an example of Jung's statement: "The indwelling of the Holy Ghost, the third Divine Person, in man, brings about a Christification of many."[27]

27. Jung, *Psychology and Religion,* CW 11, par. 758.

ὁ αἰων παῖς ἐστι παίζων
πεττεύων παιδος ἡ βασιληίη
τελεσφόρος διελαύνων τους
σκοτεινους του κοσμου τόπους
και ὡς αστηρ αναλαμπων εκ
του βαθους ὁδηγει παρ᾽
ἡελίοιο πυλας και δημον
ονειρων

(Transcription by Edward Edinger)

# Index

115

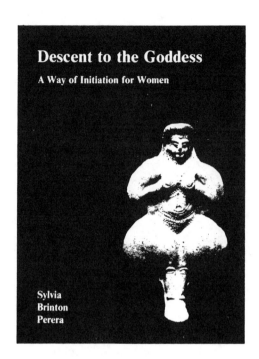

**Descent to the Goddess**

A Way of Initiation for Women

Sylvia
Brinton
Perera

**6. Descent to the Goddess: A Way of Initiation for Women.**
Sylvia Brinton Perera (New York). ISBN 0-919123-05-8. 112 pp.

A highly original and provocative book about women's freedom and the need for an inner, female authority in a masculine-oriented society.

Combining ancient texts and modern dreams, the author, a practising Jungian analyst, presents a way of feminine initiation. Inanna-Ishtar, Sumerian Goddess of Heaven and Earth, journeys into the underworld to Ereshkigal, her dark "sister," and returns. So modern women must descend from their old role-determined behavior into the depths of their instinct and image patterns, to find anew the Great Goddess and restore her values to modern culture.

Men too will be interested in this book, both for its revelations of women's essential nature and for its implications in terms of their own inner journey.

"The most significant contribution to an understanding of feminine psychology since Esther Harding's *The Way of All Women*."—**Marion Woodman,** Jungian analyst and author of *Addiction to Perfection, The Pregnant Virgin* and *The Owl Was a Baker's Daughter.*

**Addiction to Perfection**

The Still Unravished Bride

A Psychological Study by
Marion Woodman

## 12. Addiction to Perfection: The Still Unravished Bride.
Marion Woodman (Toronto). ISBN 0-919123-11-2. 208 pp.

"This book is about taking the head off an evil witch." With these words Marion Woodman begins her spiral journey, a powerful and authoritative look at the psychology and attitudes of modern woman.

The witch is a Medusa or a Lady Macbeth, an archetypal pattern functioning autonomously in women, petrifying their spirit and inhibiting their development as free and creatively receptive individuals. Much of this, according to the author, is due to a cultural one-sidedness that favors patriarchal values—productivity, goal orientation, intellectual excellence, spiritual perfection, etc.—at the expense of more earthy, interpersonal values that have traditionally been recognized as the heart of the feminine.

Marion Woodman's first book, *The Owl Was a Baker's Daughter: Obesity, Anorexia Nervosa and the Repressed Feminine,* focused on the psychology of eating disorders and weight disturbances.

Here, with a broader perspective on the same general themes, she continues her remarkable exploration of women's mysteries through case material, dreams, literature and mythology, in food rituals, rape symbolism, Christianity, imagery in the body, sexuality, creativity and relationships.

"It is like finding the loose end in a knotted mass of thread. . . . What a relief! Somebody knows!"—**Elizabeth Strahan,** *Psychological Perspectives.*

# Studies in Jungian Psychology
# by Jungian Analysts

*Quality Paperbacks*

*Prices and payment in $US (except in Canada, $Cdn)*

1. **The Secret Raven: Conflict and Transformation**
Daryl Sharp (Toronto). ISBN 0-919123-00-7. 128 pp. $15

2. **The Psychological Meaning of Redemption Motifs in Fairy Tales**
Marie-Louise von Franz (Zürich). ISBN 0-919123-01-5. 128 pp. $15

3. **On Divination and Synchronicity: The Psychology of Meaningful Chance**
Marie-Louise von Franz (Zürich). ISBN 0-919123-02-3. 128 pp. $15

4. **The Owl Was a Baker's Daughter: Obesity, Anorexia and the Repressed Feminine** Marion Woodman (Toronto). ISBN 0-919123-03-1. 144 pp. $16

5. **Alchemy: An Introduction to the Symbolism and the Psychology**
Marie-Louise von Franz (Zürich). ISBN 0-919123-04-X. 288 pp. $18

6. **Descent to the Goddess: A Way of Initiation for Women**
Sylvia Brinton Perera (New York). ISBN 0-919123-05-8. 112 pp. $15

7. **The Psyche as Sacrament: A Comparative Study of C.G. Jung and Paul Tillich** John P. Dourley (Ottawa). ISBN 0-919123-06-6. 128 pp. $15

8. **Border Crossings: Carlos Castaneda's Path of Knowledge**
Donald Lee Williams (Boulder). ISBN 0-919123-07-4. 160 pp. $16

9. **Narcissism and Character Transformation: The Psychology of Narcissistic Character Disorders**
Nathan Schwartz-Salant (New York). ISBN 0-919123-08-2. 192 pp. $18

10. **Rape and Ritual: A Psychological Study**
Bradley A. Te Paske (Santa Barbara). ISBN 0-919123-09-0. 160 pp. $16

11. **Alcoholism and Women: The Background and the Psychology**
Jan Bauer (Montreal). ISBN 0-919123-10-4. 144 pp. $16

12. **Addiction to Perfection: The Still Unravished Bride**
Marion Woodman (Toronto). ISBN 0-919123-11-2. 208 pp. $18pb/$20hc

13. **Jungian Dream Interpretation: A Handbook of Theory and Practice**
James A. Hall, M.D. (Dallas). ISBN 0-919123-12-0. 128 pp. $15

14. **The Creation of Consciousness: Jung's Myth for Modern Man**
Edward F. Edinger (Los Angeles). ISBN 0-919123-13-9. 128 pp. $15

15. **The Analytic Encounter: Transference and Human Relationship**
Mario Jacoby (Zürich). ISBN 0-919123-14-7. 128 pp. $15

16. **Change of Life: Dreams and the Menopause**
Ann Mankowitz (Ireland). ISBN 0-919123-15-5. 128 pp. $15

17. **The Illness That We Are: A Jungian Critique of Christianity**
John P. Dourley (Ottawa). ISBN 0-919123-16-3. 128 pp. $15

18. **Hags and Heroes: A Feminist Approach to Jungian Psychotherapy with Couples** Polly Young-Eisendrath (Philadelphia). ISBN 0-919123-17-1. 192 pp. $18

19. **Cultural Attitudes in Psychological Perspective**
Joseph L. Henderson, M.D. (San Francisco). ISBN 0-919123-18-X. 128 pp. $15

20. **The Vertical Labyrinth: Individuation in Jungian Psychology**
Aldo Carotenuto (Rome). ISBN 0-919123-19-8. 144 pp. $16

**44. The Dream Story**
Donald Broadribb (Baker's Hill, Australia). ISBN 0-919123-45-7.  256 pp.  $18

**45. The Rainbow Serpent: Bridge to Consciousness**
Robert L. Gardner (Toronto). ISBN 0-919123-46-5. 128 pp.  $15

**46. Circle of Care: Clinical Issues in Jungian Therapy**
Warren Steinberg (New York). ISBN 0-919123-47-3. 160 pp.  $16

**47. Jung Lexicon: A Primer of Terms & Concepts**
Daryl Sharp (Toronto). ISBN 0-919123-48-1. 160 pp.  $16

**48. Body and Soul: The Other Side of Illness**
Albert Kreinheder (Los Angeles). ISBN 0-919123-49-X. 112 pp.  $15

**49. Animus Aeternus: Exploring the Inner Masculine**
Deldon Anne McNeely (Lynchburg, VA). ISBN 0-919123-50-3. 192 pp.  $18

**50. Castration and Male Rage: The Phallic Wound**
Eugene Monick (Scranton, PA). ISBN 0-919123-51-1. 144 pp.  $16

**51. Saturday's Child: Encounters with the Dark Gods**
Janet O. Dallett (Seal Harbor, WA). ISBN 0-919123-52-X. 128 pp.  $15

**52. The Secret Lore of Gardening: Patterns of Male Intimacy**
Graham Jackson (Toronto). ISBN 0-919123-53-8. 160 pp.  $16

**53. The Refiner's Fire: Memoirs of a German Girlhood**
Sigrid R. McPherson (Los Angeles). ISBN 0-919123-54-6. 208 pp.  $18

**54. Transformation of the God-Image: Jung's *Answer to Job***
Edward F. Edinger (Los Angeles). ISBN 0-919123-55-4. 144 pp.  $16

**55. Getting to Know You: The Inside Out of Relationship**
Daryl Sharp (Toronto). ISBN 0-919123-56-2. 128 pp.  $15

**56. A Strategy for a Loss of Faith: Jung's Proposal**
John P. Dourley (Ottawa). ISBN 0-919123-57-0. 144 pp.  $16

**57. Close Relationships: Family, Friendship, Marriage**
Eleanor Bertine (New York). ISBN 0-919123-58-9. 160 pp.  $16

**58. Conscious Femininity: Interviews with Marion Woodman**
Introduction by Marion Woodman (Toronto). ISBN 0-919123-59-7. 160 pp.  $16

**59. The Middle Passage: From Misery to Meaning in Midlife**
James Hollis (Philadelphia). ISBN 0-919123-60-0. 128 pp.  $15

**60. The Living Room Mysteries: Patterns of Male Intimacy, Book 2**
Graham Jackson (Toronto). ISBN 0-919123-61-9. 144 pp.  $16

**61. Chicken Little: The Inside Story *(A Jungian Romance)***
Daryl Sharp (Toronto). ISBN 0-919123-62-7. 128 pp.  $15

**62. Coming To Age: The Croning Years and Late-Life Transformation**
Jane R. Prétat (Providence, RI). ISBN 0-919123-63-5. 144 pp.  $16

**63. Under Saturn's Shadow: The Wounding and Healing of Men**
James Hollis (Philadelphia). ISBN 0-919123-64-3. 144 pp.  $16

*Discounts: any 3-5 books, 10%; 6 books or more, 20%*
*Add Postage/Handling: 1-2 books, $2; 3-4 books, $4; 5-9 books, $8; 10 or more, free*

*Write or phone for free Catalogue of over 70 titles*

**INNER CITY BOOKS**
**Box 1271, Station Q, Toronto, ON M4T 2P4, Canada**          (416) 927-0355

P 12 the epochal man, whose life
inaugurates a new epoch, a new age